THE PEOPLE OF
BUCHAN

1600 - 1799

By
David Dobson

CLEARFIELD

Printed for Clearfield Company by
Genealogical Publishing Company
Baltimore, Maryland
2018

ISBN 9780806358734

INTRODUCTION

The district of Buchan lies in Aberdeenshire on the north east coast of Scotland. The people of Buchan found in this book lived in Fraserburgh and Peterhead, and the surrounding parishes of Cruden, Longside, Lonmay, St Fergus, Crimond, Strichen, Tyrie, Pitsligo, Deer, and Aberdour during the seventeenth and eighteenth centuries.. The economy of Buchan then was largely based on agriculture, fishing, and to a lesser extent whaling. Fraserburgh and Peterhead were port and market towns with trading links to Scandinavia, the Baltic countries, and the Netherlands, with the occasional voyage to the Americas. Nearby Aberdeen, however, dominated the local voyages to America and the West Indies. The earliest Buchan ship bound for America was the Star of Peterhead in 1668.

The major families to be found in Buchan were Keith, Forbes, Gordon, Ogilvie, Fraser, Gordon, Hay, and Leslie. Emigration occurred from Buchan to various destinations in northern Europe, especially in the seventeenth century, and to the Americas in the eighteenth century. Probably the most prominent of Buchan emigrants who ventured to northern Europe was James Keith from Peterhead, who became a Field Marshal in the service of King Frederick the Great of Prussia, while Buchan inhabitant Hugh Mercer, son of the minister of Pitsligo, became a hero of the American Revolution.

This book is based on research into manuscripts and published sources mainly located in Aberdeen and Edinburgh, including the Aberdeen City Archives, the 1667 Valuation Roll of Aberdeenshire, and The Peterhead Whaling Trade.

David Dobson

Dundee, Scotland, 2018.

THE PEOPLE OF BUCHAN, 1600-1799

REFERENCES

ABR = Aberdeen Burgess Roll

ACA = Aberdeen City Archives

AJ = Aberdeen Journal

ASC = Aberdeen Sheriff Court

ASW = Aberdeen Shore Works

AUL = Aberdeen University Library

BBR = Banff Burgess Roll

CCVC Colonial Clergy of Virginia & Carolinas

CRA = Cess Roll of Aberdeen

EMA = Emigrant Ministers to America, 1690-1811

F   = Fasti Ecclesiae Scoticanae

FPA = Fulham Papers, American

GAR = Rotterdam Archives

HSP = Historical Society of Pennsylvania

HP = History of Peterhead

JAB = Jacobites of Aberdeen and Banff

JNES = Jacobites of North East Scotland

MCA = Marischal College, Aberdeen

MSC = Miscellany of the Spalding Club

NARA = National Archives, Records Administration

NRS = National Records of Scotland

OSA = Old Statistical Accounts, 1791-1794

THE PEOPLE OF BUCHAN, 1600-1799

PPA = Pollable Person, Aberdeenshire, 1696

PWT = The Peterhead Whaling Trade

RGS = Register of the Great Seal of Scotland

RPCS = Register Privy Council of Scotland

SAA = Society of the Advocates in Aberdeen

SEC = Scottish Episcopal Clergy, 1689-2000

SM = Scots Magazine

SNC = Smuggling Story of the Northern Shores

TNA = The National Archives, Kew

TWY = The Whaling Years, Peterhead, 1788-1893

UPC = History of the United Presbyterian Church

VMHB Virginia Magazine of History and Biography

VRA = Valuation Roll of Aberdeenshire in 1667.

THE PEOPLE OF BUCHAN, 1600-1799

ABERDEEN, ALEXANDER, of Cairnbulg, testament, 30 May 1768, Comm. Aberdeen. [NRS]

ABERDEEN, JAMES, a labourer in Newton, Cruden, a Jacobite in 1745. [JNES.1]

ABERNETHIE, WILLIAM, of Crimondgate, a contract, 19 May 1655. [NRS.G1.67.13]

ABERNETHY, WILLIAM, of Crimondgate, testament, 11 October 1793, Comm. Aberdeen. [NRS]

ADAMSON, JOHN, sr., in Strichen, testament, 30 June 1809. [NRS.Comm. Aberdeen]

ADAMSON, WILLIAM, in Fraserburgh, deeds, 1696, [NRS.RD2.79.848; RD3.84.469]

ADAMSON, ..., a merchant in Fraserburgh, a deed, 1696. [NRS.RD4.78.272]

ADAMSON, ..., schoolmaster in Peterhead from 1788. [OSA]

AIRDES, WILLIAM, a skipper in Peterhead, arrived in Aberdeen on 30 July 1663. [ASW.491]

AIRTH, JOHN, a merchant in Peterhead, testament, 9 March 1751, Comm. Aberdeen. [NRS]

AITKEN, ROGER, Episcopalian priest of Cruden Bay in 1782. [SEC.525]

ALEXANDER, CHARLES, in Strathend of Cruden, testament, 16 July 1817, Comm. Aberdeen. [NRS]

ALEXANDER, GEORGE, a white-fisherman in Bullars of Buchan, Cruden, 1696. [PPA.2]

ALEXANDER, GILBERT, a white-fisherman in Bullars of Buchan, Cruden, 1696. [PPA.2]

THE PEOPLE OF BUCHAN, 1600-1799

ALEXANDER, GILBERT, a tailor in Peterhead, testament, 6 April 1756, Comm. Aberdeen. [NRS]

ALEXANDER, GILBERT, a tanner and shipowner in Peterhead, husband of Katherine Robertson, ca1800. [SAA.388]

ALEXANDER, JAMES, a white-fisherman in Bullars of Buchan, Cruden, 1696. [PPA.2]

ALEXANDER, JOHN, in Pitsligo, a letter, 1736. [NRS.RH15.1.145]

ALEXANDER, ..., master of the Providence of Cruden, trading between Dundee and Aberdeen in 1752. [AJ.248]

ALLAN, JOHN, in Fraserburgh, a member of the Aberdeenshire Militia in 1807. [ACA.AS.AMI.6.1.1]

ALLAN, JOHN, a maltman in Pitsligo, testament, 29 July 1735, Comm. Aberdeen. [NRS]

ALLARDYCE, WILLIAM, master of the Margaret of Peterhead arrived in Aberdeen on 14 August 1665. [ASW.14]

ALLARDYCE, WILLIAM, in Corbshill, New Deer, testament, 23 January 1784, Comm. Aberdeen. [NRS]

ANDERSON, AGNES, born 1750, widow of Reverend Andrew Youngson minister of Aberdour, died in the Manse of Strichen in 1825. [AJ.22.5.1825]

ANDERSON, ALEXANDER, a merchant in Fraserburgh, deeds, 1696. [NRS.RDD2.79.830; RD4.78.804]

ANDERSON, ALEXANDER, in Abbey of Deer, testament, 8 June 1762, Comm. Aberdeen. [NRS]

ANDERSON, ALEXANDER, in Strichen, 1763-1767. [NRS.RH15.27.87]

ANDERSON, ALEXANDER, a surgeon in Peterhead, testament, 8 October 1806, Comm. Aberdeen. [NRS]

THE PEOPLE OF BUCHAN, 1600-1799

ANDERSON, ANN, in New Leeds of Strichen, testament, 3 May 1821, Comm. Aberdeen. [NRS]

ANDERSON, BASIL, born 1750 in Selkirk, minister at Old Deer from 1779 until his death on 16 June 1797, testament, 12 February 1798, Comm. Aberdeen. [NRS][OSA][F.6.217]

ANDERSON, GEORGE, husband of Mary Troley, in Aberdour, a member of the Aberdeenshire Militia in 1806. [ACA.AS.AMI.6.1.1]

ANDERSON, ISOBEL, widow of Thomas Milne, in Auchiries, testament, 16 August 1760, Comm. Aberdeen. [NRS]

ANDERSON, JAMES, master of the Marie of Peterhead, a deed, 1697. [NRS.RD4.41.39]

ANDERSON, JAMES, minister at Rathen, testament, 19 February 1741, Comm. Aberdeen. [NRS]

ANDERSON, JAMES, master of the Earl of Fife of Peterhead, from Peterhead to London in 1783. [AJ.1869]

ANDERSON, Dr JAMES, in St Kitts, later in Midmiln of Cruden, 20 December 1800. [RGS.132.34.35]

ANDERSON, JAMES, sr., a merchant in Peterhead, testament, 20 February 1823, Comm. Aberdeen. [NRS]

ANDERSON, JOHN, a farmer in Greens of Strichen, testament, 5 January 1804, Comm. Aberdeen. [NRS]

ANDERSON, THOMAS, born 29 January 1710 son of Reverend James Anderson minister at Rathen, graduated MA from King's College, Aberdeen, in 1728, minister at Aberdour from 1734 until 1765. Husband of Agnes Auchenleck, daughter of Alexander Auchenleck minister of Fraserburgh, parents of James {died in St Croix in 1759}, Elizabeth, Anna, Margaret, Mary, Alexander, Samuel, Thomas, William, Agnes, Christian, and Magdalene. [F.6.210] [Aberdour gravestone]

THE PEOPLE OF BUCHAN, 1600-1799

ANDERSON, WILLIAM, a white-fisherman in Longhaven, Cruden, 1696. [PPA.2]

ANDERSON, WILLIAM, born 1789, a landsman from Raffan, aboard the whaling ship the Oscar of Aberdeen bound for Greenland, was shipwrecked and drowned off Aberdeen on 1 April 1813. [Nigg grave]

ANDERSON, Reverend WILLIAM, born 1746, died in the Manse of St Fergus in 1823. [AJ.5.3.1823]; testament, 18 July 1823, Comm. Aberdeen. [NRS]

ANDERSON, WILLIAM, a book-seller in Peterhead, testament, 9 July 1823, Comm. Aberdeen. [NRS]

ANDERSON, Dr, from Strichen, a physician in Jamaica in 1784. [HSP.1582.29B]

ANGUS, GEORGE, a tailor in Longside, a Jacobite in 1745. [JNES.2]

ANGUS, WILLIAM, a labourer in Newton of Cruden, a Jacobite in 1745. [JNES.2]

ANNAND, ALEXANDER, a sailor aboard the whaling ship Robert of Peterhead off Greenland and the Davis Straits in 1794. [NRS.E508.94.8.10]

ANNAND, JAMES, was served heir to Alexander Annand, son of Captain Robert Annand, in house and lands of Oldclochtow, in Slains, on 1 April 1668. [NRS.S/H]

ANNAND, ROBERT, an apprentice of the Robert of Peterhead whaling off Greenland or the Davis Straits in 1791. [NRS.E508.91.8]; a steersman, as above, in 1794. [NRS.E508.94.8.10]

ANNAND, ..., proprietor of Haddo in Crimond in 1790s. [OSA]

THE PEOPLE OF BUCHAN, 1600-1799

ARBUTHNOTT, ALEXANDER, born 1687, son of Nathaniel Arbuthnott of Peterhead, a dyer in Peterhead, a Jacobite in 1715. [JNES]; testament, 2 November 1742, Comm. Aberdeen. [NRS]

ARBUTHNOT, ANN, fourth daughter of James Arbuthnot a merchant in Peterhead, testament, 11 May 1791, Comm. Aberdeen. [NRS]

ARBUTHNOT, CHRISTIAN, in Kirkton of Peterhead, daughter of James Arbuthnot in Rora, testament, 31 December 1796, Comm. Aberdeen. [NRS]

ARBUTHNOTT, CHRISTIAN, widow of Thomas Fraser a shipmaster in Peterhead, testament, 24 February 1816, Comm. Aberdeen. [NRS]

ARBUTHNOTT, JAMES, a skipper in Peterhead, testament, 2 November 1742, Comm. Aberdeen. [NRS]

ARBUTHNOTT, JAMES, a merchant in Peterhead, co-owner of the Robert of Peterhead a two masted brig, active in whaling off Spitzbergen after 1788. [NRS.E08.91.8]

ARBUTHNOTT, JAMES, a merchant in Peterhead in 1781. [NRS.GD84.2.70]

ARBUTHNOTT, JAMES, of Dens, born 1741, died in Peterhead in 1823. [AJ.19.3.1823]

ARBUTHNOT, JAMES, born 1757, late postmaster of Peterhead, died there in 1829. [AJ.9.2.1829]

ARBUTHNOT, JAMES, a white-thread manufacturer in Peterhead, second son of James Arbuthnot a merchant there, testament, 1791, Comm. Aberdeen. [NRS]

ARBUTHNOT, JOHN, land owner of Haddo, parish of Crimond, 1770. [NRS.E106.36.5]

THE PEOPLE OF BUCHAN, 1600-1799

ARBUTHNOT, JOHN, a white thread manufacturer in Peterhead, second son of James Arbuthnot a merchant there, testament, 11 May 1791. Comm. Aberdeen. [NRS]

ARBUTHNOT, MARGARET, relict of Robert Kilgour, in Peterhead, testament, 27 September 1805, Comm. Aberdeen. [NRS]

ARBUTHNOTT, MARJORY, born 1747, daughter of Nathaniel Arbuthnott of Hatton, died in Peterhead in 1825. [AJ.3.5.1825]

ARBUTHNOTT, ROBERT, in Peterhead, in 1741, reference in deed. [NRS.GD67.173]

ARBUTHNOTT, ROBERT, a merchant in Peterhead, in Thomas Arbuthnott's testament, 1745, Comm. Edinburgh. [NRS]

ARBUTHNOTT, THOMAS, of Peterhead and Rora, born 1681, eldest son of Nathaniel Arbuthnott and his wife Elspet Duncan, a Jacobite in 1715, husband of Christian Young, parents of James and 7 daughters, died on 24 March 1762. [JAB.17/217][CRA.149] [JRA.211][JNES.3]

ARBUTHNOTT, THOMAS, the younger, born 1727, a merchant and bailie of Peterhead, a bond, 1732; a Jacobite in 1745, escaped to France, a. [NRS.CS271.25454] skipper trading to America and the West Indies, died in Peterhead on 1 December 1773. [JNES.3]

ARBUTHNOTT, THOMAS, a surgeon from Peterhead who settled in Virginia where he died on 10 November 1742, testament, 1745, Comm. Edinburgh. [NRS]

ARBUTHNOTT, THOMAS, a skipper in Peterhead, master of the Clementina of Peterhead trading with Danzig in 1751-1752, [NRS.E504.1.4]; master of the Marischal Keith of Peterhead at Venice in 1754, [AJ.368]; a sasine, 1791. [NRS.RS.Aberdeen.1006]; testament, 7 January 1780, Comm. Aberdeen. [NRS]

THE PEOPLE OF BUCHAN, 1600-1799

ARBUTHNOTT, THOMAS, a merchant in Peterhead in 1781. [NRS.GD84.2.70]; co-owner of the herring buss Polly of Peterhead in 1792, [NRS.E508.94.9.56]; testament, 6 January 1794, Comm. Aberdeen. [NRS]

ARBUTHNOTT, THOMAS, jr., co-owner of the herring buss Polly of Peterhead in 1792. [NRS.E508.94.9.56]

ARBUTHNOTT, THOMAS, of Nether Kinmundy, died in Peterhead in 1826. [AJ.11.3.1826]

ARBUTHNOTT, DALGARNO, and Company, woollen cloth manufacturers in Peterhead, 1790s. [OSA]

ARBUTHNOTT, GRANT, and Company, cotton cloth manufacturers in Peterhead, 1790s. [OSA]

AUCHENLECK, ALEXANDER, minister at Fraserburgh from 1707 until his death on 11 September 1753, husband of Elizabeth Fraser, parents of Agnes, Elizabeth, and George. [F.6.222]

BAGRIE, WILLIAM, a labourer at Gateside, Cruden, a Jacobite in 1745. [JNES.3]

BAIN, ALEXANDER, a seaman in Findhorn, died at sea on 22 January 1786. [Aberdour gravestone]

BANKS, ALEXANDER, MA, minister at Peterhead from 1674 until 1682. [F.6.231]

BANNERMAN, ALEXANDER, a minister in Peterhead, was deposed in 1716. [JAB.222]

BANNERMAN, WILLIAM, a schoolmaster in Peterhead, testament, 31 August 1814, Comm. Aberdeen. [NRS]

BARCLAY, ALEXANDER, was educated at King's College, Aberdeen, graduated MA in 1668, minister at Peterhead from 1682 to 1695, an Episcopalian and a Jacobite, deposed in 1716, later preacher in Longate, Peterhead, husband of Margaret Burnet. [F.6.231][SEC.533]

BARCLAY, ANDREW, in Broadlyhill, Slains, testament, 6 August 1782, Comm. Aberdeen. [NRS]

BARCLAY, ANN, wife of Captain John Thomson in Peterhead, was served heir to her brother James Barclay of Cairness who died on 4 January 1765, on 19 March 1766. [NRS.S/H]

BARCLAY, GEORGE, a shipmaster of Peterhead, arrived in Aberdeen on 29 October 1661. [ASW.471]

BARCLAY, GEORGE, from Cairnes, Peterhead, settled in Jamaica before 1727. [AUL.MS1160.5.2/11]

BARCLAY, GEORGE, heir to his grandfather Andrew Hay, in lands in Longside, Peterhead, 23 October 1741. [NRS.GD67.173]

BARCLAY, GILBERT, in Cruden, a Jacobite in 1745. [JNES.4]

BARCLAY, JOHN, a minister at Cruden, a petition, 1689. [NRS.CH12.12.2]

BARCLAY, JOHN, son of Reverend Adam Barclay, Episcopalian priest of Cruden Bay from 1678 to 1691, and of Peterhead from 1696 to 1714. [SEC.525/533][F.4.231]

BARLAS, WILLIAM, minister of Whitehill [Antiburgher] Church from 1779 to 1797, settled in New York as a classics teacher and book-seller, died 7 January 1817. [UPC.137]

BARTLET, JAMES, at the Mill of Auchmedden, died February 1732, husband of Margaret Shand, died June 1721. [Aberdour gravestone]

BAXTER, ROBERT, surgeon of the Robert of Peterhead whaling off Greenland or the Davis Straits in 1791. [NRS.E508.91.8]

THE PEOPLE OF BUCHAN, 1600-1799

BAXTER, WILLIAM, a skipper in Fraserburgh in 1632. [ASC.2.323]

BAXTER, WILLIAM, from Dundee, married Elizabeth Birnie or Donaldson, a widow, in Fraserburgh, on 17 December 1797. [NRS.CH12.32.2]

BEATON, JAMES, in Gardenend of Saak of Deer, testament, 23 March 1778. Comm. Aberdeen. [NRS]

BELL, ROBERT, a skipper in Aberdour, a deed, 1696. [NRS.RD4.78.276]

BIRNIE, ANDREW, a sailor in Peterhead, testament, 12 June 1753, Comm. Aberdeen. [NRS]

BLACKHALL, JAMES, husband of Christian Gibson, in Fraserburgh, a member of the Aberdeenshire Militia in 1805. [ACA.AS.AMI.6.1.1]

BIRNIE, ALEXANDER, a Sergeant of Colonel Hay's Regiment, married Eleanora, daughter of William Milne a mason, in Fraserburgh on 20 November 1798. [Fraserburgh Episcopal records]

BIRNIE, ALEXANDER, in Kinbog, Fraserburgh, testament, 24 March 1803, Comm. Aberdeen. [NRS]

BIRNIE, BATHIA, in Fraserburgh, widow of William Walker in the Mains of Techmuiry, testament, 20 March 1815, Comm. Aberdeen. [NRS]

BIRNIE, BETTY, in Strichen in 1761. [NRS.RH15.27.78]

BIRNIE or DAVISON, ELIZA, a widow in Fraserburgh, married William Baxter, a widower from Dundee, on 17 December 1797. [Fraserburgh Episcopal records]

BIRNIE, SAMUEL, a merchant in Fraserburgh, testament, 12 March 1763, Comm. Aberdeen. [NRS]

THE PEOPLE OF BUCHAN, 1600-1799

BIRNIE, WILLIAM, a skipper in Peterhead, testament, 23 January 1788, Comm. Aberdeen. [NRS]

BISSET, ALEXANDER, a skipper in Fraserburgh, a deed, 1682. [NRS.RD4.51.302]; in 1696, [PPA.1]; master of the Hope of Peterhead from Inverness bound for Holland on 4 May 1685. [NRS.E72.11.11]

BISSET, ALEXANDER, a skipper in Peterhead, a deed, 1701. [NRS.RD4.89.138]

BISSET, JOHN, a merchant in Fraserburgh, a deed, 1696. [NRS.RD4.79.109]

BISSET, WILLIAM, a merchant in Fraserburgh, a bond, 1652. [NRS.GD195.104.2]

BLACK, ALEXANDER, born 1680, farmer in Woodhead, died 15 February 1743, father of Christen, Margaret, and Samuel, died 1721. [Aberdour gravestone]

BLACK, JAMES, a shipmaster in Peterhead, log book of the schooner Naughton, 1814-1815. [NRS.CS235.C28.1]

BLACKIE, WILLIAM, a farmer in Netherton, married Margaret Cooper, in Fraserburgh on 28 December 1799. [Fraserburgh Episcopal records]

BLAIR, ..., master of the St Andrew of Glasgow arrived in Peterhead with tobacco from Maryland in July 1749. [AJ.82]

BODIE, JOHN, a skipper in Peterhead, testament, 24 March 1812, Comm. Aberdeen. [NRS]

BOYN, MARJORY, servant o Eilliam Hay minister ar Cruden, testament, 2 June 1747, Comm. Aberdeen. [NRS]

BRADY, WILLIAM, a labourer from Rathen, a Jacobite in 1745. [JNES.5]

THE PEOPLE OF BUCHAN, 1600-1799

BREADIE, ALEXANDER, a white fisher at Bullars of Buchan, Cruden, in 1696. [PPA.2]

BREADIE, ALEXANDER, a white fisher at Wardhill, Cruden, in 1696. [PPA.2]

BREADIE, GEORGE, a white fisher at Bullars of Buchan, Cruden, in 1696. [PPA.2]

BREADIE, GEORGE, a white fisher at Wardhill, Cruden, in 1696. [PPA.2]

BREADIE, JOHN, a white fisher at Bullars of Buchan, Cruden, in 1696. [PPA.2]

BREADIE, ROBERT, a white fisher at Bullars of Buchan, Cruden, in 1696. [PPA.2]

BREBNER, JOHN, a merchant in Peterhead, a petition, 1746. [NRS.RH18.3.94]

BRIDGE, ALLAN, a skipper in Fraserburgh, master of the Barbara of Fraserburgh from Inverness to Rotterdam on 4 April 1682, arrived in Inverness from Holland on 29 January 1686; master of the Janet of Fraserburgh from Findhorn to Holland on 7 October 1689, returned to Findhorn from Holland on 21 February 1690, from Findhorn to Holland on 16 April 1690, returned to Findhorn from Holland on 15 October 1690; arrived in Aberdeen from Norway on 12 October 1691; [NRS.E72.11.5/6/12/15/16/17; E72.1.20]; deeds, 1679, 1680, 1687, [NRS.RD3.46.76; RD2.53.184; RD3.67.71].

BROCKIE, or BROWN, JANET, in Fraserburgh, testament, 3 November 1814, Comm. Aberdeen. [NRS]

BRODIE, ALEXANDER, a fisherman in the service of the Earl of Erroll, who absconded in 1684. [RPCS.VIII.495]

BRODIE, JOHN, master of the Mary of Cruden trading between

11

THE PEOPLE OF BUCHAN, 1600-1799

Aberdeen and Muldo in 1743; master of the <u>Mary of Peterhead</u>, trading between Peterhead and Dunkirk in 1751, between Aberdeen and London in 1752, shipwrecked and drowned off the Kirk of Slains when bound from Caithness to Aberdeen in 1752. [AJ.193/194/228/230/243/253.][NRS.E504.1.1/4]; a skipper in Peterhead, testament, 19 August 1772, Comm. Aberdeen. [NRS]

BRODIE, JOSEPH, from Leith, a Captain in the Royal Navy, residing in Peterhead, testament, 12 August 1816, Comm. Aberdeen. [NRS]

BRODIE, WILLIAM, a sailor in Bullersbuchan, in 1761. [NRS.S/H]

BROWN, ANDREW, a sailor from the Mill of Achiell, Strichen, died upon the <u>St Andrew</u> at Darien in 1698, testament, 1707, Comm. Edinburgh. [NRS.GD406.1.Bundle 159.p4/18]

BROWN, ANDREW, a merchant in Fraserburgh, a Jacobite in 1715. [JNES.5]

BROWN, DAVID, MA, minister at Peterhead from 1721 until 1725. [F.6.232]

BROWN, GEORGE, a skipper in Peterhead, testament, 25 February 1734, Comm. Aberdeen. [NRS]

BROWN, GEORGE, born 1738, in Quarryhead, died 25 January 1777, husband of Margaret Gordon. [Aberdour gravestone]

BROWN, JAMES, born 1662, graduated MA from Edinburgh University in 1687, minister at Aberdour from 1697 until his death on 31 July 1732. Husband of Margaret Forbes, parents of John – later minister at Longside. [F.6.210] [Aberdour gravestone]

BROWN, JOHN, educated at Marischal College, Aberdeen, from 1610 to 1614, minister at New Deer from 1620. [F.6.218]

BROWN, JOHN, a seaman in Fraserburgh in 1696. [PPA.2]

THE PEOPLE OF BUCHAN, 1600-1799

BROWN, JOHN, in Easter Crichie, later in Glack, testament, 4 December 1753, Comm. Aberdeen. [NRS]

BROWN, WILLIAM, master of the Two Brothers of Fraserburgh trading with Bergen and Danzig in 1749. [NRS.E504.1.3]

BRUCE, ALEXANDER, a wright in Auchlin, Aberdour, testament, 5 December 1765, Comm. Aberdeen. [NRS]

BRUCE, JAMES, at Scotsmill of Craig of Inverugie, Longside, 20 December 1620. [ASC]

BRUCE, JEAN, widow of Robert Montgomery, in Old Deer, inventory, 20 August 1818, Comm. Aberdeen. [NRS]

BRUCE, JOHN, born 1794, a seaman from Fraserburgh, aboard the whaling ship the Oscar of Aberdeen bound for Greenland, was shipwrecked and drowned off Aberdeen on 1 April 1813. [Nigg grave]

BRUCE, JOSEPH, a merchant in Fraser burgh, married Margaret Murdoch, in Fraserburgh, on 15 September 1796. [Fraserburgh Episcopal records]

BRUCE, ROBERT, MA, minister at Old Deer from 1674 until 1681. [F.6.216]

BRUCE, WILLIAM, a skipper in Peterhead, a deed in 1661. [NRS.RD4.2.267]

BRUCE, WILLIAM, a sailor from Peterhead, who died aboard the St Andrew at Darien in 1698, testament, 1707, Comm. Edinburgh. [NRS]

BRUCE, WILLIAM, born 1718, tenant in Mill of Auchlin, died 26 January 1795, husband of Isabella Bruce, born 1719, died 30 November 1798. [Aberdour gravestone]

THE PEOPLE OF BUCHAN, 1600-1799

BRUCE, WILLIAM, born 1762, a cooper in Fraserburgh, died 16 July 1829, husband of Elizabeth Cowie, born 1772, died 15 October 1859. [Fraserburgh Kirkton gravestone]

BRUCE, WILLIAM, born 1738, late in Mosside of Allathen, died 18 June 1767. [New Deer gravestone]

BRYDIE, ALEXANDER, a skipper in Peterhead, testament, 8 May 1753, Comm. Aberdeen. [NRS]

BRYDIE, JOHN, a skipper in Peterhead, testament, 8 May 1753, Comm. Aberdeen. [NRS]

BRYDIE, PATRICK, master of the ....of Faithly/Fraserburgh, arrived in Aberdeen on 24 April 1597. [ASW.28]

BUCHAN, ALEXANDER, [1], born 1785, a seaman from Inverallochy, aboard the whaling ship the Oscar of Aberdeen bound for Greenland, was shipwrecked and drowned off Aberdeen on 1 April 1813. [Nigg grave]

BUCHAN, ALEXANDER, [2], born 1788, a harpooner from Peterhead, aboard the whaling ship the Oscar of Aberdeen bound for Greenland, was shipwrecked and drowned off Aberdeen on 1 April 1813.

BUCHAN, GEORGE, a sailor in Peterhead, on trial for perjury in 1768. [AJ.1051]

BUCHAN, GEORGE, born 1784, a harpooner from Peterhead, aboard the whaling ship the Oscar of Aberdeen bound for Greenland, was shipwrecked and drowned off Aberdeen on 1 April 1813.

BUCHAN, JEAN, in Ludquharn, Old Deer, testament, 29 April 1803, Comm. Aberdeen. [NRS]

BUCHAN, JOHN, a labourer in Hillhead of Cruden, a Jacobite in 1745. [JNES.5]

THE PEOPLE OF BUCHAN, 1600-1799

BUCHAN, JOHN, master of the Speedwell of Cairnbulg trading with Kirkcaldy in 1751. [NRS.E504.1.4]

BUCHAN, JOHN, born 1768, a seaman from Inverallochy, aboard the whaling ship the Oscar of Aberdeen bound for Greenland, was shipwrecked and drowned off Aberdeen on 1 April 1813. [Nigg grave]

BUNYAN, JOHN, born 1751, minister of Whitehill [Antiburgher] Church from 1798, died 20 December 1821. [UPC.137]; husband of Janet Ireland. [New Deer gravestone]

BURNET, ADAM, in Fraserburgh, was admitted as a burgess of Aberdeen on 29 March 1611. [ABR]

BURNET, GEORGE, a skipper in Peterhead, master of the sloop Peggy of Peterhead in 1788, [AJ.2095]; testament, 4 August 1789, Comm. Aberdeen. [NRS]

BURNETT, GEORGE, husband of Isabel Lunan, in Fraserburgh, a member of the Aberdeenshire Militia in 1807. [ACA.AS.AMI.6.1.1]

BURNET, JAMES, in Fraserburgh, was admitted as a burgess of Aberdeen on 29 March 1611. [ABR]

BURNETT, ROBERT, of Crimond, an advocate, 1661. [NRS.GD42.B8-9]

BURNETT, ..., of Dens, near Stewartfield, parish of Deer, established a bleachfield there in 1783. [OSA]

BURNS, JOHN, husband of Margaret Davidson, in Fraserburgh, a member of the Forfarshire Militia in 1804. [ACA.AS.AMI.6.1.1]

BUTHLAW, ALEXANDER, a whitefisher in Wardhill, Cruden, in 1696. [PPA.2]

BUTHLAW, GILBERT, a whitefisher in Wardhill, Cruden, in 1696. [PPA.2]

THE PEOPLE OF BUCHAN, 1600-1799

BUTTER, PATRICK, in Overtoun of Memsie, Rathen, testament, 8 June 1787, Comm. Aberdeen. [NRS]

CADGER, PETER, husband of Mary Pennie, in Fraserburgh, a member of the Aberdeenshire Militia in 1806. [ACA.AS.AMI.6.1.1]

CAMERON, HUGH, steersman on the Robert of Peterhead whaling off Greenland or the Davis Straits in 1791. [NRS.E508.91.8]; also, in 1794. [NRS.E508.94.8/10]

CAMPBELL, ARCHIBALD, in the Mill of Ardendraught, Cruden, a sasine, 18 April 1721. [NRS.RH8.315]

CARDNO, JOHN, son of William Cardno in Fraserburgh, was educated at Marischal College in Aberdeen, from 1792 to 1795, later a minister in Portsoy, Banffshire. [MCA.375]

CARDNO, WILLIAM, a house carpenter in Fraserburgh, married Eliza Cumine, in Fraserburgh on 21 April 1793. [Fraserburgh Episcopal records]

CARGILL, THOMAS, of Auchtydonald, parish of Longside, husband of Anna Abercromby in 1662. [VRA.208]

CARLE, ALEXANDER, a whitefisher in Rathen, in 1696. [PPA.1]

CARLE, GILBERT, a whitefisher in Cairnbulg, Rathen, in 1696. [PPA.1]

CARLE, JAMES, a whitefisher in Cairnbulg, Rathen, in 1696. [PPA.1]; born 1650, a fisher at the Seatoun of Cairnbulg, died in June 1761, [Lonmay gravestone]

CARLE, JAMES, accused of murder at Auchtydonald, Longside, in 1800. [NRS.JC26.1800.10]

CARL, JOHN, a fisherman in Cairnbulg, testament, 5 April 1822. [NRS.CC1]

THE PEOPLE OF BUCHAN, 1600-1799

CARLE, THOMAS, a whitefisher in Cairnbulg, Rathen, in 1696. [PPA.1]

CARNEGIE, JOHN, surgeon aboard the whaling ship Robert of Peterhead off Greenland and the Davis Straits in 1794. [NRS.E508.94.8.10]

CARNO, WILLIAM, died 15 January 1733, [Crimond gravestone]

CATTO, JAMES, a shipmaster in Fraserburgh, and a Jacobite in 1715. [JAB.217][JNES.7]

CATTO, JAMES, a house carpenter in Fraserburgh, a Jacobite in 1745. [JNES.6]

CENTER, ALEXANDER, a merchant in Fraserburgh, testament, 13 September 1822, Comm. Aberdeen. [NRS]

CHALMERS, ALEXANDER, born 1730, eldest son of Provost William Chalmers of Aberdeen, late of Antigua, died in Peterhead, Aberdeenshire, on 9 January 1778. [AJ.1567]; in Peterhead, testament, 15 April 1778, Comm. Aberdeen. [NRS]

CHALMERS, JOHN, second son of William Chalmers minister at Boyndie, was educated at King's College, Aberdeen, in 1655, minister at Peterhead from 1664 until 1674, died after October 1678, husband of Margaret Keith. [F.6.231]

CHALMERS, JOHN, born 1746, died 13 February 1825, husband of Isabell Scott, born 1746, died 6 August 1826. [Aberdour gravestone]

CHALMERS, WILLIAM, master of the Mary of Peterhead trading between Christiansands, Newcastle, Aberdeen, in 1751, [NRS.E504.1.4]

CHEIN, ..., a baillie of Fraserburgh, 1696. [NRS.RH9.2.51]

CHEIN, GEORGE, a sailor in Fraserburgh, a Jacobite n 1745. [JNES.7]

THE PEOPLE OF BUCHAN, 1600-1799

CHEYNE, JAMES, Episcopalian priest of Rathen from 1695 TO 1703. [SEC.533]

CHEYNE, ROBERT, in Netherhill of St Fergus, testament, 2 August 1745, Comm. Aberdeen. [NRS]

CHIVAS, JAMES, a skipper in Fraserburgh, master of the Margaret of Fraserburgh in 1751, [AJ.165]; trading between, Aberdeen Bergen, Bo'ness, Veere, Belfast and Kirkcaldy in 1750-1752, [NRS.E504.1.3/4]; 1751, [AJ.165]; testament, 17 February 1759, Comm. Aberdeen. [NRS]

CHIVAS, ROBERT, in Upper Adiel of Strichen, testament, 31 July 1815, Cmm. Aberdeen. [NRS]

CHRISTIE, JAMES, a skipper in Fraserburgh, papers, 1741-1748. [NRS.GD164.347]; in 1782, [NRS.S/H]

CHRISTIE, JAMES, born 1792, a seaman from Peterhead, aboard the whaling ship the Oscar of Aberdeen bound for Greenland, was shipwrecked and drowned off Aberdeen on 1 April 1813. [Nigg grave]

CHRISTIE, JOHN, in the Mains of Artamford, New Deer, testament, 9 May 1817, Comm. Aberdeen. [NRS]

CHRISTIE, WILLIAM, master of the Elisa of Fraserburgh trading with Veere in 1750, [NRS.E504.1.3]; master of the Elizabeth of Fraserburgh, trading between Veere, Newcastle, Kirkcaldy, and Flekkefiord in1751-1752. [NRS.E504.1.4][AJ.209]; a skipper in Fraserburgh, husband of Barbara Clark, testament, 1778, Comm. Aberdeen. [NRS]

CHRISTIE, ..., master of the Mary of Fraserburgh trading between Newcastle and Fraserburgh in 1751. [AJ.208]

CHRISTY, ..., master of the Elizabeth of Fraserburgh trading between Veere and Aberdeen in 1752. [AJ.209/253]

CLERK, ALEXANDER, a whitefisher in Wardhill, Cruden, in 1696. [PPA.1]

THE PEOPLE OF BUCHAN, 1600-1799

CLARK, ..., master of the Happy Isobel of Fraserburgh in Aberdeen, 1755. [AJ.413]

CLARK, BARBARA, widow of William Christie a shipmaster in Fraserburgh, testament, 24 February 1778, Comm. Aberdeen. [NRS]

CLARK, CHRISTIAN, wife of Alexander Robertson a wheelwright in Peterhead, testament, 12 December 1772, Comm. Aberdeen. [NRS]

CLARK, GEORGE, graduated MA at King's College, Aberdeen, in 1611, minister at Aberdour from 1614 until his death on 18 August 1644, husband of Jane Ogston, parents of George, William, Christian, Margaret, and Jean. [F.6.209][Aberdour gravestone]

CLERK, GILBERT, graduated MA from Edinburgh University in 1646, minister at New Deer from 1654 until 1681, husband of Jean Clerk, parents of Mary, Janet, and Jean. [F.6.218]

CLERK, GILBERT, a whitefisher in Longhaven, Cruden, in 1696. [PPA.2]

CLARK, JAMES, in Netherhill, St Fergus, 1796. [NRS.CS96.43]

CLERK, JOHN, a mariner in Fraserburgh in 1696. [PPA.2]

CLUB, ALEXANDER, master of the Pretty Peggy of Fraserburgh trading with Christiansands , Norway, in 1750. [NRS.E504.1.3]

CLUB, ALEXANDER, born 1767 in Fraserburgh, a merchant, was naturalised in South Carolina on 25 September 1802. [NARA.M1183/1]

CLUB, ALEXANDER, a skipper in Fraserburgh, husband of Jean Taylor, a sasine, 1790. [NRS.RS.Aberdeen.892]

CLUB, JAMES, skipper of the Salton of Fraserburgh in 1767. [AJ.1026]

19

COCK, GILBERT, in the Mill of Inverchumrie, Longside, a jury-man, 23 June 1596. [ASC]

COCK, WILLIAM, a fresh or green man aboard the whaling ship Robert of Peterhead off Greenland and the Davis Straits in 1794. [NRS.E508.94.8.10]

COCKBURN, JOHN, minister at Old Deer from 1681 until 1683. [F.6.216]

COGLE, WILLIAM, a mariner in Fraserburgh, a deed, 1714. [NRS.RD4.115.101]

COOK, ALEXANDER, a white-fisher in Cairnbulg, Rathen, in 1696. [PPA.1]

COOK, JAMES, born 1754, a farmer in Cairnmurnen, Tyrie, died 21 March 1837, husband of Rebekah Urquhart, born 1749, did 17 December 1829. [Aberdour gravestone]

COOK, JOHN, son of Thomas Cook and his wife Beatrice Dickie in Cocklaw, Peterhead, a servant in Ull, Latvia, died in September 1589. [MSC.II.23]

COOK, Reverend PATRICK, in Auchiries, testament, 30 September 1728, Comm. Aberdeen. [NRS]

CORDINER, JOHN, in Burnhillock, Cruden, testament, 3 June 1811, Comm. Aberdeen. [NRS]

CORDINER, ROBERT, born 1670, a skipper in Peterhead, died on 29 December 1712. [Peterhead gravestone]

CORDINER, ROBERT, master of the Good Intention of Peterhead trading between Aberdeen and Trontheim in 1743. [NRS.E504.1.1]

CORDINER, ..., master of the Friendship of Peterhead, trading between Peterhead and Fraserburgh in 1755. [AJ.398]

THE PEOPLE OF BUCHAN, 1600-1799

CORDINER, ..., master of the Success of Peterhead, bound via Stromness for Virginia in 1758. [AJ.536]

CORDINER, Mrs, born 1748, widow of Reverend Charles Cordiner, died in Peterhead in 1834. [AJ.15.11.1834]

CORMACK, GEORGE, a fresh or green man on the Robert of Peterhead whaling off Greenland or the Davis Straits in 1791. [NRS.E508.91.8]

CORMACK, WILLIAM, master of the Mary of Slains trading with Kirkcaldy in 1749-1750. [NRS.E504.1.3]

CORMACK, WILLIAM, a sailor aboard the whaling ship Robert of Peterhead off Greenland and the Davis Straits in 1794. [NRS.E508.94.8.10]

COUTIE, ALEXANDER, treasurer of the Sea Box of Fraserburgh, a deed, 1714. [NRS.RD4.114.44]

COW, ALEXANDER, a farmer in Peterhead, testament, 19 September 1812, Comm. Aberdeen. [NRS]

COW, WILLIAM, a carpenter in Peterhead, later in Newton of Kinmundy, testament, 3 December 1816. [NRS]

COWIE, ALEXANDER, a skipper in Fraserburgh, treasurer of the Sea Box of Fraserburgh, a deed in 1700. [NRS.RD2.83.746]

COWIE, JAMES, master of the Mary of Fraserburgh, a charter-party for a voyage from Dingwall to Leith, 2 March 1702. [NRS.GD305.1.147.53]

COWY, JEROM, master of the .....of Faithly/Fraserburgh bound for Flanders on 16 September 1596; arrived in Aberdeen from Norway on 19 May 1597. [ASW.24/28]

COWIE, JOHN, in Kinbeam, died 13 September 1715, father of John and James. [Aberdour gravestone]

THE PEOPLE OF BUCHAN, 1600-1799

COYLE, WILLIAM, a seaman in Fraserburgh, in 1696. [PPA.2]

CRAB, WILLIAM, a sailor on the Robert of Peterhead whaling off Greenland or the Davis Straits in 1791. [NRS.E508.91.8]

CRAIG, ALEXANDER, born 1777 in Peterhead, a crewman of the herring buss Polly of Peterhead in 1792. [NRS.E508.94.9.56]

CRAIG, ALEXANDER, an apprentice aboard the whaling ship Robert of Peterhead off Greenland and the Davis Straits in 1794. [NRS.E508.94.8.10]

CRAIG, ANDREW, line manager of the Robert of Peterhead whaling off Greenland or the Davis Straights in 1791. [NRS.E508.91.8]

CRAIK, ALEXANDER, a mariner in Fraserburgh, testament, 15 June 1742, Comm. Aberdeen. [NRS]

CRAIK, ALEXANDER, master of the Success of Fraserburgh trading with Lisbon and Bumblefjord in 1752. [NRS.E504.1.4]

CRAIK, JOHN, a merchant in Fraserburgh, testament, 25 February 1731, Comm. Aberdeen. [NRS]

CRAIK, WILLIAM, master of the Friendship of Fraserburgh trading between Kirkcaldy and Aberdeen in 1752. [NRS.E504.1.4]

CRAICK, ..., master of the Prince George of Fraserburgh, trading between Gothenburg and Aberdeen in 1755. [AJ.385]

CRIGHTON, ALEXANDER, in the Mill of Auchmeddan, husband of Anne Brodie born 1736, died 15 May 1774. [New Deer gravestone]

CRICHTON, WILLIAM, in Clackriach, Old Deer, testament, 29 July 1783, Comm. Aberdeen. [NRS]

CROMERY, WILLIAM, a seaman in Peterhead in 1696. [PPA.1]

THE PEOPLE OF BUCHAN, 1600-1799

CRUICKSHANK, ALEXANDER, a bailie in Peterhead, testament, 20 December 1722, Comm. Aberdeen. [NRS]

CRUDEN, JAMES, a skipper in Fraserburgh, testament, 30 June 1783, Comm. Aberdeen. [NRS]

CRUDEN, JEAN, in Rosehearty, testament, 29 August 1775, Comm. Aberdeen. [NRS]

CRUDEN, JOHN, a merchant in Aberdeen, residing in Newton of Strichen, testament, 19 May 1740, Comm. Aberdeen. [NRS]

CRUICKSHANK, ALEXANDER, in the Mains of Iden, testament, 22 February 1748, Comm. Aberdeen. [NRS]

CRUICKSHANK, GEORGE, a Jacobite in Fraserburgh in 1715. [JNES.8]

CRUICKSHANK, JAMES, a farmer at Toukshill, New Deer, testament, 6 May 1814, Comm. Aberdeen. [NRS]

CRUICKSHANK, Dr JOHN, a surgeon in Fraserburgh, a Jacobite in 1745. [JNES.8]

CRUICKSHANK, ROBERT, of Banchrie, the factor of Pitsligo, 1695. [NRS.165.232/234]

CUI, ALEXANDER, a seaman in Fraserburgh in 1696. [PPA.2]

CUI, JAMES, a seaman in Fraserburgh in 1696. [PPA.2]

CUMINE, WILLIAM, minister at Tyrie from 1762 until 1772. [F.6.245]

CUMING, ALEXANDER, was granted the lands of Crimond on 22 May 1693. [NRS.SIG.1.27.130 J2]; testament, 30 July 1723, and 15 January 1734, Comm. Aberdeen. [NRS]

CUMING, ALEXANDER, Episcopalian priest of Peterhead from 1719 to 1721. [SEC]

THE PEOPLE OF BUCHAN, 1600-1799

CUMING, ALEXANDER, a merchant in Greenbrae, Cruden, testament, 16 March 1782, Comm. Aberdeen. [NRS]

CUMING, ELIZABETH, daughter of George Cuming of Pittuly, testament, 30 December 1800, Comm. Aberdeen. [NRS]

CUMMING, GEORGE, a seaman in Aberdour in 1696. [PPA.1]

CUMMING, JOHN, a seaman in Aberdour in 1696. [PPA.2]

CUMMING, JAMES, of Brunthill, husband of Grizel Martin. [VRA.207]

CUMING, WILLIAM, minister at Rathen, testament, 21 October 1800, Comm. Aberdeen. [NRS]

CUMMINE, JOHN GORDON, of Pitlurg, owner of Leask in the parish of Slains in 1770. [NRS.E106.36.5]

CUMMINE, WILLIAM, of Pitsligo in 1770. [NRS.E106.36.5]

CUMMINE, ..., in Kinnonmont, Lonmay, 1791. [NRS.E326.9.15]

DALGARNO, ALEXANDER, a merchant in Peterhead, testament, 22 July 1777, Comm. Aberdeen. [NRS]

DALGARNO, ALEXANDER, son of Alexander Dalgarno a manufacturer in Peterhead, was apprenticed to Charles Walker a merchant in Aberdeen, for 5 years, 25 June 1785. [ACA]; a merchant in Peterhead, a testament, 27 August 1793, Comm. Aberdeen. [NRS]

DALGARNO, JOHN, a merchant in Auchmunzie, New Deer, a Jacobite in 1745. [JNES.9]

DALGARNO, JOHN, in Old Deer, was impressed into Colonel Leighton's regiment, in 1757. [ACA.as.amil.2.17]

DALGARNO, THOMAS, in Longside, testament, 19 January 1762, Comm. Aberdeen. [NRS]

THE PEOPLE OF BUCHAN, 1600-1799

DALGARNO, WILLIAM, Episcopalian priest of St Fergus from 1678 to 1696. [SEC.534]

DALLACHY, JOHN, a book-seller in Peterhead, testament, 15 May argaret

DALRYMPLE, JOHN, a merchant in Fraserburgh, testament, 19 June 1812, Comm. Aberdeen. [NRS]

DALRYMPLE, WILLIAM, a surgeon, son of James Dalrymple in Fraserburgh, died in Trelawney, Jamaica, on 31 March 1860. [AJ.9.5.1860]

DALRYMPLE, ..., master of the Tibby of Fraserburgh trading between Fraserburgh and Danzig in 1784. [AJ.1916]

DARG, WILLIAM, a seaman in Fraserburgh in 1696. [PPA.2]

DARGUE, A., a sailor in Peterhead, died before 1760. [NRS.S/H]

DARGUE, ANDREW, a boatbuilder in Peterhead, testament, 5 February 1805, Comm. Aberdeen. [NRS]

DAVIDSON, JAMES, born 1725, in the Mains of Bruxie, died 19 May 1781, husband of Margaret Watt, born 1724, died in Old Deer on 5 June 1823, parents of George Davidson, born 1764, a merchant in Old Deer, died 4 April 1833. [New Deer gravestone]

DAVIDSON, WILLIAM, master of the William of Peterhead, arrived in Aberdeen from Leith in 1613. [ASW.78]

DAVIDSON, WILLIAM, a merchant in Peterhead, a deed, 1696. [NRS.RD4.78.1390]

DAVIDSON, WILLIAM, born 1792, a seaman from Fraserburgh, aboard the whaling ship the Oscar of Aberdeen bound for Greenland, was shipwrecked and drowned off Aberdeen on 1 April 1813. [Nigg grave]

DAVIDSON, ..., master of the Rebecca of Peterhead from Fraserburgh to Aberdeen in 1758. [AJ.542]

THE PEOPLE OF BUCHAN, 1600-1799

DAWNIE, ALEXANDER, a seaman in Rosehearty, Pitsligo, in 1696. [PPA.2]

DAWNIE, JAMES, a seaman in Aberdour, in 1696. [PPA.2]

DAWNIE, JAMES, a seaman in Rosehearty, Pitsligo, in 1696. [PPA.2]

DAWNIE, WILLIAM, a seaman in Rosehearty, Pitsligo, in 1696. [PPA.2]

DAWSON, JOHN, in the Mains of Iden, testament, 15 August 1748, Comm. Aberdeen. [NRS]

DICK, ALEXANDER, a labourer in Turnilove, Cruden, a Jacobite in 1745. [JNES.10]

DICK, GEORGE, a merchant in Peterhead, a deed, 1696.

DONALD, ROBERT, master of the Mary of Peterhead trading between Newcastle, Peterhead, and Aberdeen in 1754-1755. [AJ.354/371]

DOUGALL, WILLIAM, a skipper in Fraserburgh, a deed, 1714. [NRS.RD2.103/2.402]

DOUGLAS, ALEXANDER, minister at New Deer from 1650 until deposed in 1653. [F.6.218]

DOWNIE, BARBARA, daughter of Alexander Downie a weaver in Aberdour, testament, 13 January 1748, Comm. Aberdeen. [NRS]

DOWNIE, JAMES, a sailor from Peterhead, died aboard the Unicorn at Darien in 1698, testament, 1707, Comm. Edinburgh. [NRS]

DOWNIE, JAMES, a merchant in Fraserburgh, testaments, 14 November 1743 and 18 August 1746, Comm. Aberdeen. [NRS]

26

THE PEOPLE OF BUCHAN, 1600-1799

DOWNIE, WILLIAM, born 1701, died 14 November 1780, husband of Janet Watt, born 1704, lived on the shore of Pennan, died 1 January 1775. [Aberdour gravestone]

DRUMMOND, JOHN, a mariner, later master, aboard the Isabel of Fraserburgh, a deed, 1701, [NRS.RD4.89.930]; a deed, 1707. [NRS.RD2.94.931]; a deed, 1714. [NRS.RD3.143.650]; a skipper in Fraserburgh, husband of Isobel Bisset, testament, 1729, Comm. Aberdeen. [NRS]; master aboard the Isobel of Fraserburgh bound from the Hermans Islands off Norway was captured by a French privateer in 1708. [ACA.APB.2]

DRUMMOND, WILLIAM, a skipper in Fraserburgh, testament, 16 November 1727, Comm. Aberdeen. [NRS]

DUFF, Admiral, land owner of Logie, in the parish of Crimond in 1770. [NRS.E106.36.5]; Duff of Fetteresso, heritor of Logie in 1790s. [OSA]

DUGUID, MARGARET, widow of Andrew Henry a shipmaster in Peterhead, testament, 29 May 1795, Comm. Aberdeen. [NRS]

DUNBAR, ANDREW, son of Robert Dunbar in Peterhead, married Catherine Sutherland, daughter of Robert Sutherland, in Elgin in December 1667, a process of divorce in 1677. [NRS.CC8.6.20]

DUNBAR, ARCHIBALD, a Writer to the Signet, in the Manse of Rathen, testament, 2 December 1809, Comm. Aberdeen. [NRS]

DUNBAR, JAMES, at the Mill of Rethen, testament, 1 March 1728, Comm. Aberdeen, [NRS]

DUNBAR, WILLIAM, Episcopalian priest of Peterhead from 1719 to 1721. [SEC]

DUNBAR, WILLIAM, husband of Janet Black, in Peterhead, an army reservist in 1804. [ACA.AS.AMI.6.1.1]

THE PEOPLE OF BUCHAN, 1600-1799

DUNCAN, ALEXANDER, husband of Barbara Hay, in Collieston, Slains, a member of the Aberdeenshire Militia in 1807. [ACA.AS.AMI.6.1.1];

DUNCAN, JOHN, a dyer in Broadgait, Peterhead, a sasine. [NRS.RH1.2.515]; testament, 7 November 1727, Comm. Aberdeen. [NRS]

DUNCAN, ROBERT, a sailor aboard the Mary of Peterhead, was shipwrecked and drowned off the Kirk of Slains, Aberdeenshire, in November 1752. [AJ.253]

DUNCAN, ROBERT, in Old Deer, was discharged from military duty in 1757. [ACA.as.amil.2.17]

DUNCAN, ROBERT, an apprentice of the Robert of Peterhead whaling off Greenland or the Davis Straits in 1791. [NRS.E508.91.8]

DUNCAN, WILLIAM, a merchant in Peterhead, a testament, 23 January 1783, Comm. Aberdeen. [NRS]

DUNN, WILLIAM, born 1782, a seaman from Raffan, aboard the whaling ship the Oscar of Aberdeen bound for Greenland, was shipwrecked and drowned off Aberdeen on 1 April 1813.

DURHAM, JOHN, Episcopalian priest of Fraserburgh from 1768 to 1788. [SEC.527]; a letter, 1768. [NRS.CH12.23.1337]

DUTHIE, ROBERT, a whitefisher in Inverallochy, Rathen, testament, 21 August 1806. [NRS.CC1]

DUTHIE, WILLIAM, a white-fisher in Rathen in 1696. [PPA.1]

DUTHIE, WILLIAM, a white-fisher in Inverallochy, Rathen, testament, 21 August 1806, Comm. Aberdeen. [NRS]

THE PEOPLE OF BUCHAN, 1600-1799

DUTHIE, WILLIAM, husband of Christine Robertson, in Peterhead, a member of the Aberdeenshire Militia in 1808. [ACA.AS.AMI.6.1.1]

ELMSLIE, GEORGE, master of the Two Brothers of Fraserburgh from Antigua via Stromness to Holland in September 1751. [AJ.199]; trading with Sinfure in 1752. [NRS.E504.1.4]

ELPHINSTONE, ..., master of the Phoenix of Fraserburgh a charter party of 1691, for a voyage from Orkney to Leith. [NRS.E41.21.18]

ELRICK, ROBERT, in Dens, Longside, a testament, 1775, Comm. Aberdeen. [NRS]

FAIRHOLME, or FERME, CHARLES, born 1567 near Edinburgh, graduated MA from Edinburgh University in 1587, minister at Fraserburgh from 1598 until his death on 24 September 1617. [F.6.221]

FALCONER, ALEXANDER, a sailor in Fraserburgh, a Jacobite in 1745. [JNES.12]

FALCONER, WILLIAM, a wheelwright in Old Deer, testament, 11 December 1792, Comm. Aberdeen. [NRS]

FARQUHAR, ALEXANDER, minister of Slains in 1790s [OSA]

FARQUHAR, ANDREW, born 1678, in the land of Haddo, died 16 August 1747, his spouse Marjorie Mitchell, born 1681, died 10 June 1758. [Crimond gravestone]

FARQUHAR, JAMES, in Tyrie, 1707-1709. [NRS.CH12.12.21][F.6.245]

FARQUHAR, ROBERT, MA, minister at Peterhead from 1726 until 1738. [F.6.232]

FARQUHAR, THOMAS, born 1740, farmer in Pitnacalder, died 18 January 1791, husband of Isobel Murray, born 1745, died 20

August 1793, parents of Catherine and Margaret. [Aberdour gravestone]

FARQUHARSON, MARY, in Fraserburgh, testament, 14 February 1782, Comm. Aberdeen. [NRS]

FERGUSON, ALEXANDER, a skipper in Peterhead, testament, 26 January 1744, Comm. Aberdeen. [NLS]

FERGUSON, ALEXANDER, a skipper in Peterhead, master of the Magdalene of Peterhead, trading between Gothenburg and Peterhead in 1754, [AJ.354]; was admitted as a burgess of St Andrews in 1765. [St Andrews Burgess Roll]

FERGUSON, JAMES, of Pitfour, land-owner of Adziel, parish of Strichen, also in parish of Longside, 1770. [NRS.E106.36.5]

FERGUSON, WILLIAM, Captain of the artillery company of the Peterhead Volunteers, 1799-1801. [NRS.GD44.47.45/4]

FERRIER, JAMES, a sailor in Fraserburgh, a Jacobite in 1745. [JNES.15]

FERRIER, JOHN, a seaman in Bullersbuchan, Cruden, in 1696. [PPA.2]

FINDLATOR, CUTHBERT, of Fraserburgh, letter, 3 June 1619. [ACL.165]

FINDLATOR, GEORGE, an Excise Officer in Peterhead, a Jacobite in 1715. [JNES.13]

FINDLATOR, GEORGE, a cooper in Fraserburgh, and Rebecca Durham, were married in Fraserburgh on 23 February 1800. [Fraserburgh Episcopal records]

FINLAY, THOMAS, a skipper in Colliston, Slains, 1696. [PPA.2]

FINDLAY, EIZABETH, in Fraserburgh, testament, 27 January 1747, Comm. Aberdeen. [NRS]

THE PEOPLE OF BUCHAN, 1600-1799

FINDLAY, JAMES, born 1718, farmer in Windyheads, died 14 November 1781, husband of Barbara Gordon. [Aberdour gravestone]

FINLAYSON, HENRY, a mariner in Fraserburgh, 1696. [PPA.2]

FINNIE, ANDREW, a skipper in Peterhead, in 1628. [ASC.2.310]; a skipper and bailie of Peterhead, deceased, father of Andrew, 1656. [RGS.X.534]

FLEMING, JAMES, born 1713, son of James Fleming in the Braeside of Ludquharn, 'The Laird o'Udny's Feel', died 1778. [Longside gravestone]

FORBES, ALEXANDER, of Pitsligo, was served heir to his father John Forbes in the lands and barony of Pitsligo on 1 October 1628. [NRS.Retours.Aberdeen. 209]; died 1636, husband of Joan Keith, daughter of William Keith the Earl Marischal. [Pitsligo mi]

FORBES, ALEXANDER, 2nd Lord Pitsligo, died 1677, husband of Mary Erskine, daughter of James Erskine, Earl of Buchan. [Pitsligo mi]

FORBES, ALEXANDER, 3rd Lord Pitsligo, died 1690, husband of Sophia Erskine, daughter of the Earl of Mar, parents of Charles and Jean. [Pitsligo mi]

FORBES, ALEXANDER, Lord Pitsligo, born 1678, a Jacobite in 1715, escaped to Italy, died in 1762. [JNES,14]

FORBES, ALEXANDER, Lord Pitsligo, was served heir to his father Alexander Forbes, Lord Pitsligo, on 27 April 1637. [NRS.Retours, Aberdeen.237]

FORBES, ALEXANDER, skipper of the Isobel of Fraserburgh, deeds, 1681-1682. [NRS.RD4.49.387; RD2.58.331]

FORBES, ALEXANDER, a merchant in Aberdeen, laird of Ludquharn in 1695, married Jane daughter of Alexander Galloway a merchant in Aberdeen. [VRA.206]

THE PEOPLE OF BUCHAN, 1600-1799

FORBES, ALEXANDER, a Jacobite in Fraserburgh in 1715. [JNES.14]

FORBES, ALEXANDER, a stabler in Peterhead, a Jacobite in 1745. [JNES.16]

FORBES, ALEXANDER, born 1783 in Peterhead, a merchant in Charleston, was naturalised in South Carolina on 14 December 1807. [NARA.M1183/1]

FORBES, ANDREW, a purser of the Royal Navy, later in Peterhead, testament, 2 March 1819. [NRS.CC1]

FORBES, ANNE, daughter of John Forbes of Pitsligo, and Alexander Forbes the Master of Forbes, a marriage contract, 3 June 1620. [NRS.GD52.470]

FORBES, ARTHUR, graduated MA from St Andrews in 1636, minister at Pitsligo in 1640, at Fraserburgh in 1646, died in Edinburgh on 24 August 1663, husband of Anna Copland. [F.6.222]

FORBES, BARBARA, daughter of John Forbes of Auquhorties, testament, 6 May 1746, Comm. Aberdeen. [NRS]

FORBES, CHRISTIAN, wife of James Walker at the Wardmill of Crimondgate, testament, 12 December 1772, Comm. Aberdeen. [NRS]

FORBES, ELIZABETH, in Peterhead, daughter of Captain John Forbes of Boyndlie, former wife of the late Bailie George Phillip a merchant in Banff, later wife of James Mackie of Gask, testament 1799, Comm. Aberdeen. [NRS]

FORBES, JANE, wife of Thomas Morison in Rosehearty, was served heir to her father Captain John Forbes of Boyndlie, in parts of the Barony of Pitsligo, on 4 March 1772. [NRS.S/H]

FORBES, JEAN, widow of Reverend James Leslie in St Fergus, testaments, 9 December 1754 and 12 June 1777, Comm. Aberdeen. [NRS]

THE PEOPLE OF BUCHAN, 1600-1799

FORBES, JOHN, was served heir to James Forbes of Tillegonie, Buchan, on 9 November 1649. [NRS. Retours. Aberdeen.301]

FORBES, JOHN, master of the Isabel of Peterhead in Aberdeen in 1665; master of the Andrew of Aberdeen arrived there from Leith in 1665, [ASW.511/524/531]; a skipper in Peterhead, a deed, trading between Aberdeen and Dordrecht 1669; master of the Good Intention of Peterhead trading between Aberdeen, Inverness, and Norway in 1669, [NRS.E72.11.2; E72.1.1]

FORBES, JOHN, of Pitcapel, Aberdour, born 1688, son of James Forbes of Pitcapel, graduated MA from King's College, Aberdeen, in 1707, minister at Old Deer from 1719 until his death on 20 April 1769. Husband of Margaret Hay. [F.6.216]

FORBES, JOHN, in Peterhead, in 1741, reference in deed. [NRS.GD67.173]

FORBES, JOHN, a wright at the mill of Strichen, testament, 27 June 1764, Comm. Aberdeen. [NRS]

FORBES, JOHN, of Pitsligo, Parish of Tyrie, 1770, [NRS.E106.36.5]; testament, 27 November 1781, Comm. Aberdeen. [NRS]

FORBES, JOHN, the younger, stamp-master of Peterhead in 1797. [NRS.E371.142]

FORBES, ROBERT, master of the Robert and Matthew of Peterhead trading with Bergen, Rotterdam, St Ulbes, Newcastle, Lisbon, Veere, Bumblefiord, Christiansands, and Kirkcaldy in 1749 to 1752. [NRS.E504.1.3/4][AJ.203]

FORBES, Sir SAMUEL, of Foveran, was granted the baronies of Pitsligo and of Aberdour on 22 June 1711. [NRS.GD23.4.80]

FORBES, WILLIAM, minister at Fraserburgh from 1618 until around 1640, husband of Barbara Forbes, parent of Arthur Forbes. [F.6.221]

FORBES, WILLIAM, a skipper in Peterhead in 1696. [PPA.1]

THE PEOPLE OF BUCHAN, 1600-1799

FORBES, WILLIAM, in Peterhead, letters 1766-1768. [NRS.RH15.27.101]

FORBES, W., landowner of Upper Boyndle, parish of Tyrie, 1770. [NRS.E106.36.5]

FORBES, WILLIAM, a merchant in Peterhead, 1818-1819, sederunt books [NRS.CS235.SED.BKS.f2; CS235.SEQN.F1.28]

FORBES, Mrs, of Pitsligo, Rathen, 1791. [NRS.E326.9.15]

FORREST, ELIZABETH, widow of Richard Henderson a merchant in Fraserburgh, testament, 11 June 1792, Comm. Aberdeen. [NRS]

FORREST, JOHN, master of the Neptune of Fraserburgh trading between Aberdeen and Bergen in 1743; trading between Veere and Aberdeen in 1743. [NRS.E504.1.1]; trading between Aberdeen and Arundale in 1743; between Bergen and Aberdeen in 1743; from Kirkcaldy to Aberdeen in 1743. [NRS.E540.1.1]; master of the Success of Fraserburgh trading with Lisbon in 1751, [NRS.E504.1.4][AJ.211]; master of the Pretty Peggy of William Veere, Bergen, Gothenburg, in 1751-1752, [NRS.E504.1.4]; master of the Charming Nancy of Fraserburgh trading between Aberdeen, Bumblefiord, Newcastle, and Veere in 1752. [NRS.E504.1.4]

FORREST, THOMAS, a merchant in Fraserburgh, a deed, 1693. [NRS.RD2.77.i.176]

FORSYTH, WILLIAM, born 1677, farmer in Bonnymoon, died 24 April 1765, husband of Margaret Black, born 1687, died 23 September 1744, parents of Anne, George, Margaret, and William [1720-1793] [Aberdour gravestone]

FOWLER, GEORGE, in Peterhead in 1791. [NRS.CS234, sequestration, f1.6]

FOWLER, ..., master of the Charming Nancy of Fraserburgh trading between Leith and Aberdeen in 1752. [AJ.225]

THE PEOPLE OF BUCHAN, 1600-1799

FRASER, Sir ALEXANDER, of Fraserburgh, charters, 1609, 1615. [NRS.GD1.38.6; GD67.5]

FRASER, ALEXANDER, of Phillorth, was served heir to his father Sir Alexander Fraser of Fraserburgh on 17 December 1624. [NRS.Retours.Aberdeen.185]; was granted the lands and barony of Pillorth by King Charles I on 15 March 1628. [RGS.VIII.1229]

FRASER, ALEXANDER, skipper of the Isabel of Peterhead, a deed, 1688, [NRS.RD4.63.863]; a seaman in Peterhead in 1696. [PPA.1];

FRASER, ALEXANDER, a skipper in Fraserburgh, deeds, 1681, 1696. [NRS.RD4.49.538; RD4.79.176]; master of the Good Intention of Fraserburgh trading between La Rochelle and Aberdeen in 1681. [NRS.E72.1.4]; a deed, 1701. [NRS.RD3.95.108]

FRASER, ALEXANDER, of Inverallochy, a deed, 1696. [NRS.RD4.78.797]

FRASER, ALEXANDER, was served heir to his father Alexander Fraser of Inverallochy on 7 October 1696. [NRS.S/H]

FRASER, ALEXANDER, was granted the lands of Strichen in 1732. [NRS.SIG.1.59.34]

FRASER, ALEXANDER, a skipper in Peterhead, 1735. [Peterhead Kirk Session Records, 21.9.1735]

FRASER, ALEXANDER, master of the Christina of Peterhead trading between Rotterdam and Aberdeen in 1741; trading between Aberdeen and Gothenborg in 1743; master of the Clementina of Fraserburgh trading between Hogsham and Aberdeen in 1743; from Aberdeen to Trontheim in 1743; from Gothenborg to Aberdeen in 1743; from Rotterdam to Aberdeen in 1743. [NRS.E504.1.1]; master of the Saltoun of Fraserburgh trading with St Valerie in 1749, [NRS.E504.1.3]; trading between Aberdeen, Riga, Bergen and Newcastle in 1752. [NRS.E504.1.4]; from Peterhead to Dundee in 1753. [AJ.290]

THE PEOPLE OF BUCHAN, 1600-1799

FRASER, ALEXANDER, in Peterhead, in 1741, reference in deed. [NRS.GD67.173]

FRASER, ALEXANDER, born 1720, graduated MA from Aberdeen University in 1741, minister at Fraserburgh from 1754 until his death on 17 August 1779, husband of Jean Arbuthnott, parents of Margaret and Eleanor. [F.6.222]

FRASER, ALEXANDER, was granted the lands of Strichen in 1759. [NRS.SIG.1.61.19]; there in 1770, also owner of Iden in the parish of Pitsligo in 1770. [NRS.E106.36.5]

FRASER, ALEXANDER, of Strichen, landowner of Wester and Easter Tyrie in 1770. [NRS.E106.36.5]

FRASER, ALEXANDER, master of the Peggy of Peterhead in 1787, [AJ.2078]; a skipper in Peterhead, testament, 25 April 1796, Comm. Aberdeen. [NRS]

FRASER, ALEXANDER, of Strichen, 1791. [NRS.E326.9.15]; Senator of the Colege of Justice, testament, 2 February 1792, Comm. Aberdee. [NRS]

FRASER, ALEXANDER, of Strichen, was served heir to his father Alexander Fraser of Strichen, on 5 May 1775. [NRS.S/H]

FRASER, ALEXANDER, a minister in Fraserburgh, testament, 16 June 1781, Comm. Aberdeen. [NRS]

FRASER, ALEXANDER, of Strichen, 1789. [NRS.B59.38.6.187]

FRASER, ANDREW, of Kinmundy, a burgess of Aberdeen in 1661, Sheriff Depute in 1682. [VRA.207]

FRASER, CHARLES, of Inverallochy, a deed, 1765. [NRS.GD1.661.46]; owner of Hillhead in the parish of Rathen in 1770. [NRS.E106.36.5]

THE PEOPLE OF BUCHAN, 1600-1799

FRASER, FRANCIS, of Kinmundy, in the parish of Peterhead, 1635, a burgess of Aberdeen in 1661, father of Andrew Fraser. [VRA.207][ASC]

FRASER, GEORGE, a mariner in Fraserburgh, died in February 1756. [AJ.423]

FRASER, JAMES, bailie of Fraserburgh, letter, 3 June 1619. [ACL.165]

FRASER, JAMES, master of the Hope of Fraserburgh trading between Inverness and Rotterdam in 1684-1685. [NRS.E72.11.9/10/11]

FRASER, JAMES, of Lonmay, a Jacobite in 1715, died 10 August 1729. [JNES.16]

FRASER, JAMES, of Strichen, testament, 4 January 1726, Comm. Aberdeen. [NRS]

FRASER, JAMES, of Lonmay, testament, 22 July 1730, Comm. Aberdeen. [NRS]

FRASER, JAMES, farmer at Newseat of St Fergus, testament, 13 June 1786, Comm. Aberdeen. [NRS]

FRASER, JOHN, a skipper in Fraserburgh, testament, 1757, Comm. Aberdeen. [NRS]

FRASER, JOHN, in the Mains of Cairnbulg, testament, 30 March 1733, Comm. Aberdeen. [NRS]

FRASER, MAGNUS, bailie of Fraserburgh, letter, 3 June 1619. [ACL.165]

FRASER, Mrs MARGARET, relict of Alexander Fraser if Inverallochy, a deed, 28 April 1699. [NRS.G1.38.69]

FRASER, MICHAEL, son of William Fraser, sometime in Fraserburgh later in Aberdeen, by 1619. [ACL.165]

THE PEOPLE OF BUCHAN, 1600-1799

FRASER, Sir SIMON, of Inverallochy, a sasine, 1619. [NRS.GD67.9]; was admitted as a burgess of Aberdeen on 14 August 1619. [ABR]

FRASER, Captain SIMON, a Jacobite in 1715. [JNES.16]

FRASER, SIMON, Captain of Colonel Fraser's Regiment, second son of Charles Fraser of Inverallochy, died at Quebec on 15 October 1759 of wounds received on 13 October 1759. [AJ.623]

FRASER, THOMAS, of Strichen, and his wife Christian Forbes, a sasine, 8 January 1614. [NRS.G33.6.3]; was admitted as a burgess of Aberdeen on 20 September 1619. [ABR]

FRASER, THOMAS, the apparent of Strichen, was admitted as a burgess of Aberdeen on 3 May 1625. [ABR]

FRASER, THOMAS, a skipper in London, son of Alexander Fraser a skipper in Peterhead, a sasine, 1781. [NRS.RS.Aberdeen.44]

FRASER, THOMAS, a skipper in Peterhead, a testament, 24 February 1816. [NRS.CC1]

FRASER, WILLIAM, a mariner in Fraserburgh in 1696. [PPA.2]

FRASER, WILLIAM, was served heir to his father Alexander Fraser of Inverallochy on 23 November 1698. [NRS.S/H]

FRASER, WILLIAM, of Inveralochy, a Jacobite who was killed at Sheriffmuir in 1715. [JNES.17]

FRASER, WILLIAM, of Inverallochy, testament, 4 May 1733, Comm. Aberdeen. [NRS]

FRASER, WILLIAM, of Inverallochy, a Jacobite in 1745, died in 1749. [JNES.17]

FRASER, WILLIAM, son of Alexander Fraser in Inveraven, graduated MA at Marischal College, Aberdeen, an Advocate in Aberdeen, later, in Peterhead, dead by 1760. [SAA.191]; testament, 15 January 1760. Comm. Aberdee. [NRS]

THE PEOPLE OF BUCHAN, 1600-1799

FRASER, WILLIAM, born 1742, son of Alexander Fraser, a hairdresser in Fraserburgh, graduated MA from Marischal College, Aberdeen, minister at Tyrie from 1773 until his death on 6 September 1810. Husband of Ann Wilson, parents of Sopia, Elizabeth, Alexander, and Sarah. [F.6.246]

FRASER, Dr WILLIAM, of Minzie, Rathen, 1791. [NRS.E326.9.15]

FRASER, WILLIAM, Captain of the Fraserburgh Volunteers, papers, 1798-1802. [NRS.GD44.47.44.2]

FRASER, ..., master of the Jean of Fraserburgh in 1755. [AJ.408]

FULLARTON, JOHN, the younger of Dudwick, Bowence, Cruden, a Jacobite in 1745, died 4 April 1768, his wife Mary Guthrie, born 1718, died 1805 in Aberdeen. [JNES.17]

GADIE, WILLIAM, a skipper in Peterhead, inventory, 24 November 1823. [NRS.CC1.w1191]

GARDEN, ALEXANDER, of Troup, testament, 19 November 1731, Comm. Aberdeen. [NRS]

GARDEN, ALEXANDER, of Troup, owner of Whitecairn in the parish of Rathen, also in the parish of Pitsligo, in 1770. [NRS.E106.36.5]; in the parish of Deer 1790. [OSA]; testaments, 6 March 1786, 12 March 1792, and 22 December 1794, Comm. Aberdeen. [NRS]

GARDEN, CHRISTINE, daughter of Michael Garden miller at the Mill of Cruden, process of divorce from Alexander Thom in Kinmundy who married in June 1746, divorce 4 April 1765. [NRS.CC8.6. 415]

GARDEN, FRANCIS, of Troup, a woollen cloth manufacturer at Nether Kinmundy, parish of Longside, 1790s. [OSA]

GARDEN, POOR JAMES, in Toux, testament, 2 June 1724, Comm. Aberdeen. [NRS]

THE PEOPLE OF BUCHAN, 1600-1799

GALL, ALEXANDER, a sheep-stealer from Peterhead, a felon who was transported from Aberdeen aboard the Hope bound for Virginia in June 1755. [AJ.383/388]

GARDEN, ALEXANDER, of Troup, land owner of Kinmundy, parish of Longside, 1770. [NRS.E105.36.5]

GAIRDYNE, ALEXANDER, born 1638, son of Reverend George Gardyne, graduated MA from King's College, Aberdeen, in 1652, minister at Old Deer from 1665 until 1670s, husband of Elizabeth Keith, parents of George Keith. [F.6.216]

GARIOCH, ALEXANDER, a skipper in Peterhead, a sasine, 1794. [NRS.RS.Aberdeen.1292]

GARIOCH, WILLIAM, of Torhendry, parish of Longside, husband of Elizabeth Curror, in 1668. [VRA.209]

GARIOCH, WILLIAM, a seaman in Peterhead in 1696. [PPA.1]

GAVIN, GEORGE, was educated at Marischal College, Aberdeen, in 1641, of Collietown or Collielaw in 1657, there in 1696. [VRA.208]

GEARY, ALEXANDER, born 1761 in Peterhead, mate aboard the Robert of Peterhead, later harpooner and in 1798 commander of the said whaler, master of the whaler Hope of Peterhead in 1803, died in 1809. [TWY.1][PWT.44]

GEDDES, JOHN, a seaman in Fraserburgh, a deed, 1664. [NRS.RD3.9.257]

GEDDES, JOHN, husband of Mary Cruden, in Cruden, a member of the Aberdeenshire Militia in 1804. [ACA.AS.AMI.6.1.1]

GERRARD, GORDON, from Aberdour, married Barbara Martin a servant at Ladysford, in Fraserburgh on 6 December 1798. [Fraserburgh Episcopal records]

THE PEOPLE OF BUCHAN, 1600-1799

GIBB, ALEXANDER, son of George Gibb in Slains, husband of Anna Gray, a deed, 1702. [NRS.RD3.99.2.388]

GIBB, JAMES, husband of Jean Thomson, in New Pitsligo, a member of the Aberdeenshire Militia in 1808. [ACA.AS.AMI.6.1.1]

GIBBIN, JAMES, husband of Jean Thomson, in New Pitsligo, Tyrie, a member of the Aberdeenshire Militia in 1808. [ACA.AS.AMI.6.1.1]

GILCHRIST, MARGARET, in Peterhead, widow of Lieutenant Harry Gilchrist late of the 42nd Regiment of Foot, testament, 24 May 1796, Comm. Aberdeen. [NRS]

GILL, ALEXANDER, master of the Concord of Fraserburgh trading between Bergen and Rotterdam and Aberdeen in 1742; from Rotterdam to Aberdeen in 1743. [NRS.E504.1.1]; son of Alexander Gill and his wife Barbara Urquhart in the Mains of Pitfour, a Jacobite in 1745, [JNES.18]; dead by February 1767. [AJ.996]

GILL, GEORGE, a skipper in Fraserburgh, died 17 September 1741, [Fraserburgh gravestone]; testament, 8 February 1742, Comm. Aberdeen. [NLS]

GILL, PATRICK, master of the Success of Fraserburgh in 1754. [AJ.333]

GILLES, ROBERT, a schoolmaster from Forfar, later in Cuden, a deed, 1 May 1697. [NRS.GD244.1.256]

GLEIG, JOHN, Episcopalian priest of Cruden Bay from 1785 to 1801. [SEC.525]

GORDON, ALEXANDER, town clerk of Fraserburgh, a deed, 1696. [NRS.RD3.86.87]

GORDON, ALEXANDER, of Aberdour, land owner of Aberdour and Coburty in 1770. [NRS.E106.36.5]; in Aberdour, 1791. [NRS.E326.9.15]

THE PEOPLE OF BUCHAN, 1600-1799

GORDON, ALEXANDER, a merchant in Fraserburgh, a deed, 1702. [NRS.RD3.99.1.393]

GORDON, ALEXANDER, of Aberdour, writs, 1750-1752. [NRS.GD36.77]

GORDON, ALEXANDER, of Glendeveny, land owner of Cocklaw in the parish of Peterhead in 1770. [NRS.E106.36.5]

GORDON, ALEXANDER, born 1783, a seaman from Fraserburgh, aboard the whaling ship the Oscar of Aberdeen bound for Greenland, was shipwrecked and drowned off Aberdeen on 1 April 1813. [Nigg grave]

GORDON, Mrs ANNE, in Peterhead, letters, 1755-1759. [NRS.GD67-123]; widow of John Barclay the Episcopalian minister in Peterhead, testament, 28 February 1766, Comm. Aberdeen. [NRS]

GORDON, CHARLES, of Buthlaw, owner of Invernorth, parish of Rathen in 1770. [NRS.E106.36.5]; patron of the church of Lonmay, 1790s. [OSA]

GORDON, CHARLES, land owner of Auchleuchries, parish of Cruden, 1770. [NRS.E106.36.5]; testament, 15 September 1777, Comm. Aberdee. [NRS]

GORDON, CHARLES, of Cairnies, Lonmay, 1791. [NRS.E326.9.15]

GORDON, ELIZABETH, daughter of Charles Gordon of Buthlaw, testament, 27 April 1797, Comm. Aberdeen. [NRS]

GORDON, GEORGE, at Bridgend of Deer, testament, 6 September 1733, Comm. Aberdeen. [NRS]

GORDON, JAMES, a skipper in Fraserburgh, testament, 27 December 1732, Comm. Aberdeen. [NRS]

THE PEOPLE OF BUCHAN, 1600-1799

GORDON, JAMES, a merchant in Peterhead, testament, 1 July 1756, Comm. Aberdeen. [NRS]

GORDON, JEAN, daughter of the late Dr Thomas Gordon in Peterhead, and James Jessiman, a merchant in Aberdeen, an antenuptial marriage contract, 1784. [NRS.GD1.474.9]

GORDON, JOHN, second son of Alexander Gordon of Lesmoir and his wife Anne Forbes, graduated MA from Edinburgh in 1594, minister at Aberdour from 1597 until after 1621. [F.6.212]

GORDON, JOHN, born 1685 son of the Provost of Aberdeen, educated at Marischal College, Aberdeen, 1702-1706, minister at Old Deer, from 1711 until his death in 1718, husband of [1] Barbara Gordon, [2] Jean Forbes, parents of Janet Gordon, [F.6.216]; testament, 26 January 1722, Comm. Aberdeen. [NRS]

GORDON, JOHN, born 1705, in the Mains of Auchmeddan, died 23 February 1770, husband of Janet Mudliard. [Aberdour gravestone]

GORDON, JOHN, land-owner of Balmoor in the parish of Peterhead in 1770. [NRS.E106.36.5]

GORDON, LEWIS, land-owner of Techmuiry, parish of Strichen, 1770. [NRS.E106.36.5]

GORDON, PATRICK, master of the Hope of Fraserburgh trading between Fraserburgh and Norway, 1690 -1691, [NRS.E72.1.18/19/20]; a deed, 1693, [NRS.RD2.76.165]; a deed, 1714. [NRS.RD4.114.45]

GORDON, PETER, a seaman in Fraserburgh in 1696. [PPA.2]

GORDON, ROBERT, master of the George and James of Peterhead, a charter party for a voyage from Bordeaux to Aberdeen, in 1722. [NRS.GD44.51.4557]

GORDON, THOMAS, in Buchan, a deed, 1696. [NRS.RD2.80.i.169]

THE PEOPLE OF BUCHAN, 1600-1799

GORDON, Dr THOMAS, a physician in Peterhead, husband of Jean Thomson, a deed, 1763. [NRS.GD1.474.5]; parents of John Gordon a shipmaster in London, a deed, 1770. [NRS.G1.474.7]

GORDON, THOMAS, a Consul in Fraserburgh, accounts, 1789-1797. [NRS.GD44.51.486-7]

GAMMACH, ALEXANDER, son of Alexander Gammach in New Deer, was apprenticed to James Abernethy a merchant in Aberdeen, for 4 years, 15 May 1736. [ACA]

GORDON, ALEXANDER, was served heir to his grandfather Robert Gordon of Pitlurg on 5 October 1692. [NRS.S/H]

GORDON, ROBERT, husband of Christian Forsyth born 1712, died 24 February 1750, parents of Anne, died 30 April 1750'

GORDON, BARON, & Company, cotton manufacturers in Peterhead in 1790s. [OSA]

GRANT, ARCHIBALD, husband of Mary Galloway, in Stewartfield, Old Deer, a member of the Aberdeenshire Militia in 1808. [ACA.AS.AMI.6.1.1]

GRAY, ALEXANDER, in Stonyhill of Cruden, testament, 2 December 1762, Comm. Aberdeen, [NRS]

GRAY, JAMES, master of the Lady Charlotte of Peterhead in 1784, [AJ.1884]; a skipper in Peterhead, a sasine, 1794. [NRS.RS.Aberdeen.1295]

GRAY, JAMES, steersman of the Robert of Peterhead whaling off Greenland or the Davis Straits in 1791. [NRS.E508.91.8]

GRAY, JAMES, a harpooner aboard the whaling ship Robert of Peterhead off Greenland in 1794. [NRS.E508.94.8/10]

GRAY, JAMES, a merchant in Fraserburgh, sederunt book, 1808. [NRS.CS34.SED.BKKS.4; SEQN.G.2/3]

GRAY, JOHN, a bailie of Fraserburgh, a Jacobite in 1715. [JNES.22]

THE PEOPLE OF BUCHAN, 1600-1799

GRAY, ROBERT, from Peterhead, a seaman in Dutch service, testament, Rotterdam, 3 December 1658, [GAR.ONA.217.53.199]

GRAY, ROBERT, a fresh or green man aboard the whaling ship Robert of Peterhead off Greenland and the Davis Straits in 1794. [NRS.E508.94.8.10]

GRAY, WILLIAM, a sailor of the Robert of Peterhead whaling off Greenland or the Davis Straits in 1791. [NRS.E508.91.8]

GRAY, WILLIAM, a farmer at Pitblae, married Helen Still, in Fraserburgh on 20 July 1793. [Fraserburgh Episcopal records]

GREIG, ANDREW, master of the Ann of Fraserburgh trading between Aberdeen and Bergen in 1743; from Newcastle to Aberdeen in 1743. [NRS.E504.1.1]; testament, 6 June 1751, Comm. Aberdeen. [NRS]

GREGORY, WILLIAM, master of the William of Peterhead, a deed, 1696. [NRS.RD4.85.660]

GREIG, GEORGE, a whitefisher in Bullersbuchan, Cruden, 1696. [PPA.2]

GREIG, JOHN, a skipper in Fraserburgh in 1623. [ASC.2.272]

GREIG, JOHN, a skipper in Fraserburgh, deeds, 1666, 1692. [NRS.RD4.16.691; RD4.71.911]

GREIG, THOMAS, born 1790, a seaman from Peterhead, aboard the whaling ship the Oscar of Aberdeen bound for Greenland, [Nigg grave]

GREIG, Reverend WILLIAM, born 1756, died at the Manse of Longside in 1828. [AJ.17.8.1828]

GRIG, ANDREW, an Elder of Fraserburgh, letter, 3 June 1619. [ACL.165]

THE PEOPLE OF BUCHAN, 1600-1799

GUTHRIE, ANDREW, minister at Peterhead from 1699 until 1720, died in May 1722. [F.6.231]; testaments, 12 December 1723 and 26 June 1729, Comm. Aberdeen. [NRS]

HACKET, PETER, and Elisabeth Rennie, in Rosehearty, were married in Fraserburgh on 9 September 1790. [Fraserburgh Episcopal records]

HACKET, ..., master of the Betty of Fraserburgh trading between Aberdeen and Bergen in 1790. [AJ.2225]

HADDEN, GEORGE, a skipper in London, son of Robert Hadden a weaver in Peterhead, a sasine, 1798. [NRS.RS.Aberdeen.1825]

HALKET, GEORGE, a schoolmaster of Rathen in 1714, a Jacobite in 1715, died at Memsie in 1756 and buried in Fraserburgh, husband of Janet Adamson. [JNES.23]

HAMILTON, WILLIAM, harpooner of the Robert of Peterhead whaling off Greenland or the Davis Straits in 1791. [NRS.E508.91.8]

HARDIE, JOHN, born 1698, smith in Stonybank, died 9 June 1769. [New Deer gravestone]

HARDY, ROBERT, born 1736, in Auchredie, died 22 September 1796, husband of Mary Walker. [New Deer gravestone]

HARLAW, ALEXANDER, a merchant in Fraserburgh, father of John Harlaw in Montserrat, services of heirs, 1789. [NRS]

HARLAW, JOHN, a feuar in Peterhead in 1800. [NRS.CS271.13322]

HARPER, ALEXANDER, in Fraserburgh, a charter witness on 25 August 1624. [RGS.VIII.777]

HARROW, WILLIAM, master of the Isobel of Fraserburgh was wrecked near Collieston in December 1786. [AJ.2031]

THE PEOPLE OF BUCHAN, 1600-1799

HARROW, WILLIAM, a shoemaker in Fraserburgh, married Agnes Murdoch, in Fraserburgh on 10 January 1793. [Fraserburgh Episcopal records]

HARVEY, ... of Broadland, heritor of Rattray, and Broadland in the parish of Crimond, 1791. [NRS.E326.9.15][OSA]

HAY, ALEXANDER, a whitefisher in Longhaven, Cruden, 1696. [PPA.2]

HAY, Dr ALEXANDER, owner of part of Meikle Cocklaw, parish of Peterhead in 1770. [NRS.E106.36.5]

HAY, ANDREW, a skipper in Peterhead, 1617,1634. [ASC.2.219/394]

HAY, CHRISTIAN, only daughter of Andrew Hay late bailie of Peterhead, and John Barclay, a marriage contract, 1695. [NRS.GD67.88/94]

HAY, CHARLES, advocate, a land owner in the parish of Longside in 1770. [NRS.E105.36.5]

HAY, GILBERT, in Auchirie of Cruden, testament, 10 February 1756, Comm. Aberdeen. [NRS]

HAY, JAMES, factor of Lonmay, 18 February 1730. In [NRS.CS165.603]

HAY, JOHN, of Burnthill, was served heir to his brother George Hay of Auchquharny, on 4 April 1649. [NRS.Retours.Aberdeen,295]

HAY, JOHN, a burgess of Aberdeen, was served heir to his younger brother George Hay of Auchnarne, on 5 October 1653. [NRS.Retours.Aberdeen.320]

HAY, JOHN, of Logie, was served heir to Robert Hay of Logie his brother-german in lands in the parish of Slains on 29 January 1664. [NRS.S/H]

THE PEOPLE OF BUCHAN, 1600-1799

HAY, JOHN, a seaman in Fraserburgh in 1696. [PPA.2]; a skipper in Fraserburgh, a deed, 1700. [NS.RD2.83.746]

HAY, JOHN, a skipper in Fraserburgh, a deed, 1700. [NRS.RD2.83.746]

HAY, THOMAS, minister at Crimond in 1696. [F.6.213]

HAY, WILLIAM, an Elder of Fraserburgh, letter, 3 June 1619. [ACL.165]

HAY, WILLIAM I, second son of Alexander Hay, graduated MA from Marischal College, Aberdeen, in 1623, minister at Crimond from 1628 until his death in May 1653. Father of John, William, Janet, Christian, Alexander, and Francis. [F.6.213]

HAY, WILLIAM, minister at Crimond, was served heir to his father William Hay sometime minister of Crimond, of lands in the parish of Crimond on 14 July 1658. [NRS.Retours, Aberdeen, 346]; minister at Crimond, a sasine, 1677. [NRS.GD67.85]; a deed, 1696. [NRS.RD3.85.368/387]; Husband of Margaret Meldrum, parents of John William and Thomas, he died in February 1699. [F.6.213]

HAY, WILLIAM, of Crimondgate, deeds, 1696. [NRS.RD3.84.431; 85.384-387]

HENDERSON, JOHN, born 1698, tenant in Benwalls, died 31 March 1774, husband of Jean Adamson, born 1697, died 1 August 1765. [New Deer gravestone]

HENDERSON, JOHN, born 1734, died 3 December 1810, husband of [1] Margaret Keith born 1742, died 18 July 1781, [2] Janet Smith, born 1755, died 23 January 1800. [New Deer gravestone]

HENDERSON, JOHN, born 1792, a seaman from Fraserburgh, aboard the whaling ship the Oscar of Aberdeen bound for Greenland, was shipwrecked and drowned off Aberdeen on 1 April 1813, father of Thomas Henderson later a minister in Demerara. [Newburgh gravestone, Aberdeenshire]

THE PEOPLE OF BUCHAN, 1600-1799

HENDERSON, PATRICK, an Elder of Fraserburgh, letter, 3 June 1619. [ACL.165]

HENDERSON, PETER, a merchant in Peterhead, testament, 11 June 1795, Comm. Aberdeen. [NRS]

HENDERSON, RICHARD, born 1663, sometime in Knock, died 1 June 1747. [New Deer gravestone]

HENDERSON, WILLIAM, a merchant in Fraserburgh, testament, 11 June 1792, Comm. Aberdeen. [NRS]

HENDRY, ANDREW, a skipper in Peterhead, husband of Margaret Duguid, testament, 1796, Comm. Aberdeen. [NRS]

HENDRY, GEORGE, in Old Maud, testament, 13 January 1795, Comm. Aberdeen. [NRS]

HENDRY, JEAN, in Mormond, Strichen, testament, 5 August 1795, Comm. Aberdeen. [NRS]

HENDRY, WILLIAM, a farmer at Waukmill of Ironside, husband of Elisabeth Bruce, parents of John Hendry, born 1760, died 18 January 1784, and James Hendry, born 1775, died 23 January 1784. [New Deer gravestone]

HENRYSON, HENRY, a skipper in Peterhead, dead by 1656. [RGS.X.534]

HEPBURN, ALEXANDER, born 1656 in Buchan, Episcopalian priest of St Fergus from 1703 until 1717, and of Peterhead from 1721 to his death in 1737. [SEC.534/533]; husband of Eliza Clark who died in 1703. [JNES.24]

HEPBURN, ALEXANDER, ground officer at Techmuiry, Fraserburgh, testament, 12 December 1785, Comm. Aberdeen. [NRS]

THE PEOPLE OF BUCHAN, 1600-1799

HIRD, ROBERT, master of the ....of Peterhead, in Aberdeen in 1596, 1597. [ASW.24/27]

HOGG, JAMES, born 1823, Captain of the William, son of Captain John Hogg in Peterhead, died in St Vincent on 6 October 1854. [AJ: 27.12.1854]

HOUSTOUN, ALEXANDER, master of the Success of Fraserburgh in 1755. [AJ.395]

HOUSTOUN, JOHN, Episcopalian priest of Lonmay from 1696 to 1707. [SEC.530]

HOUSTOUN, WILLIAM, a feuar in Fraserburgh, testament, 10 June 1754, Comm. Aberdeen. [NRS]

HUTCHEON, JAMES, a fisherman in the service of Sir William Keith of Ludquharn, absconded in 1683. [RPCS.VIII.119]

HUTCHEON, ROBERT, master of the Resolution of Peterhead in Aberdeen in 1752. [AJ.232]; trading with Bo'ness, Hamburg, Christiansands, Kirkcaldy, and Aberdeen in 1752-1753. [NRS.E504.1.4]

HUTCHEON, WALTER, a sailor of the Robert of Peterhead whaling off Greenland or the Davis Straits in 1791. [NRS.E508.91.8]

HUTCHIESON, ALEXANDER, born 1762 in Peterhead, a crewman of the herring buss Polly of Peterhead in 1792. [NRS.E508.94.9.56]

HUTCHESON, ANDREW, a fresh or green man aboard the whaling ship Robert of Peterhead off Greenland and the Davis Straits in 1794. [NRS.E508.94.8.10]

HUTCHISON, JOHN, in Peterhead, co-owner of the Robert of Peterhead, a two masted brig, active in whaling off Spitzbergen after 1788. [NRS.E508.91.8]

THE PEOPLE OF BUCHAN, 1600-1799

HUTCHISON, JOHN, a skipper in Peterhead, son of Robert Hutchison a skipper in Peterhead, a sasine, 1792. [NRS.RS.Aberdeen.1097]

HUTCHESON, JOHN, a sailor aboard the whaling ship Robert of Peterhead off Greenland and the Davis Straits in 1794. [NRS.E508.94.8.10]

HUTCHISON, JOHN, a fresh or green man aboard the whaling ship Robert of Peterhead off Greenland and the Davis Straits in 1794. [NRS.E508.94.8.10]

HUTCHESON, PETER, a merchant in Peterhead, testament, 1795, Comm. Aberdeen. [NRS]

HUTCHISON, ROBERT, master of the Resolution of Peterhead when bound for Danzig, was captured 50 leagues off Buchan Ness by a French privateer in 1758. [AJ.540]; a skipper in Peterhead in 1767, [AJ.991]; a sasine, 1796. [NRS.RS.Aberdeen.1614]; inventory, 5 December 1801. [NRS.CC1.w46]

IMLACH, JAMES, husband of Helen Gerrie, in New Pitsligo, a member of the Aberdeenshire Militia in 1808. [ACA.AS.AMI.6.1.1]

IRONSIDE, JOHN, in Auchreddy, New Deer, testaments, 9 August 1785, and 29 December 1786, Comm. Aberdeen. [NRS]

IRVINE, ALEXANDER, of Drum, land owner of Milhill and the Min of Crimond, in 1770. [NRS.E106.36.5][OSA]

IRVINE, ALEXANDER, born 1755, farmer in Auchmaledie, died 1 February 1805, husband of Mary Gordon, born 1761, died 29 January 1841. [New Deer gravestone]

IRVINE, W., owner of Boyndlie, parish of Tyrie, 1770. [NRS.E106.36.5]

IRVINE, ..., of Crimond, 1721, and 1726. [NRS.CS226.4882; CS236.D2.12]

THE PEOPLE OF BUCHAN, 1600-1799

IRVING, ALEXANDER, minister at Longside, a sasine, 4 November 1656. [NRS.GD33.56.26]

JACK, GEORGE, son of Alexander Jack in Gask of Cruden, was apprenticed to William Moir a cooper in Aberdeen for 6 years, 1 January 1749. [ACA]

JAFFRAY, CHARLES, a skipper in Fraserburgh in 1723. [Fraserburgh KSR,23.7.1723]

JAFFRAY, GEORGE, a feuar and farmer in Fraserburgh, testament, 7 December 1749, Comm. Aberdeen. [NRS]

JAFFRAY, JOHN, a whitefisher in Cairnbulg, Rathen, 1696. [PPA.1]

JAFFRAY, JOHN, Episcopalian priest of Lonmay from 1727 to 1768. [SEC.530]

JAFFRAY, JOHN, a wheelwright in Strichen, married Ann Pressley, in Fraserburgh on 3 August 1793. [Fraserburgh Episcopal records]

JAFFREY, PETER, a whitefisher in Cairnbulg, Rathen, 1696. [PPA.1]

JAFFREY, PETER, born 1700, tenant in Broadland, died 24 December 1756, husband of Margaret Forman, born 1680, died 28 March 1746. [Crimond gravestone]

JAFFREY, ROBERT, born 1716, died 7 January 1792, father of John Jaffrey, born 1754, died 2 October 1775. [Aberdour gravestone]

JAFFRAY, WILLIAM, MA, minister at New Deer from 1626 to 1646. [F.6.218]

JAFFREY, WILLIAM, born 1713, weaver in Tophead, St Fergus, died 16 April 1790, his wife Isobel Rob, born 1720, died 4 February 1795. [Crimond gravestone]

JAMIESON, ALEXANDER, minister at Tyrie, deeds, 1696. [NRS.RD4.78.747; RD4.79.1232]

THE PEOPLE OF BUCHAN, 1600-1799

JAMIESON, WILLIAM, master of the <u>Magdalene of Peterhead</u> trading between Peterhead, Middelburg, Lisbon, Danzig, Mandale, Kirkcaldy and Leith in 1751-1752. [AJ.257][NRS.E504.1.4]

JOHNSTON, ALEXANDER, son of George Johnstone a merchant in Old Deer, was apprenticed for 7 years to James Ewan a burgess of Aberdeen on 21 December 1654. [ACA]; a merchant in Peterhead, testament, 29 August 1769, Comm. Aberdeen. [NRS]

JOHNSTON, ALEXANDER, factor of Pitsligo, 28 February 1702. [NRS.CS165.829]

JOHNSTON, ALEXANDER, at theOvermill of Cruden, testament, 30 May 1723, Comm. Aberdeen. [NRS]

JOHNSTON, ANN, relict of John Shewan in Braco of Cruden, testament, 6 January 1808, Comm. Aberdeen. [NRS]

JOHNSTON, JAMES, son of David Johnston and his wfe Marjory Barclay in Crimond, settled in Poland by 1597. [APB]

JOHNSTON, JAMES, minister in Crimond, testament, 1796, Comm. Aberdeen. [NRS]

JOHNSTON, JOHN, son of William Johnston in Old Deer, was apprenticed to Alexander Still a butcher in Aberdeen, for 5 years, 10 January 1770. [ACA]

JOHNSTON, ROBERT, in Midmilne of Cruden, testament, 26 January 1747, Comm. Aberdeen. [NRS]

JOLLY, ALEXANDER, born 1755, Episcopalian priest of Fraserburgh from 1788 to 1838, and Bishop of Moray, died in Fraserburgh in 1838. [SEC. 527][AJ.29.6.1838]

JOLLIE, WILLIAM, in Fraserburgh, a Jacobite in 1715. [JNES.26]

KEAY, CHARLES, minister at Old Deer from 1769 until 1779. [F.6.217]

KEITH, BARBARA, daughter of William Keith in Peterhead, married John Rodgers, son of Richard Rodgers in Bo'ness, in the Scots Kirk of Rotterdam in 1709. [GAR]

KEITH, Sir ALEXANDER, of Ludquharn, parish of Peterhead, died 1666, husband of Margaret Bannerman of Elsick. [VRA.205]

KEITH, ALEXANDER, Episcopalian priest of Cruden Bay from 1719 to 1763. [SEC.525]

KEITH, ..., in 1629, minister at Peterhead from 1604 to 1605. [F.6.231]

KEITH, ANDREW, reader and session clerk of Fraserburgh, letter, 3 June 1619. [ACL.165]

KEITH, GEORGE, Episcopalian priest of Old Deer from 1683 to 1710. [SEC.532]; born 1642, son of Reverend John Keith, graduated MA from Marischal College, Aberdeen, in 1658, minister at Old Deer from 1683 until his death on 16 July 1710. Husband of [1] Mary Browne, parents of William, Margaret, Mary, [2] Sophia Ross, parents of Alexander. [F.6.216]

KEITH, GEORGE, a seaman aboard the Isobel of Fraserburgh bound from the Hermans Islands off Norway was captured by a French privateer in 1708. [ACA.APB.2]

KEITH, GEORGE, a merchant in Fraserburgh, testament, 10 March 1727, Comm. Aberdeen. [NRS]

KEITH, GEORGE, a merchant in Fraserburgh, testament, 4 June 1748, Comm. Aberdeen. [NRS]

KEITH, JAMES, born 1696 in Peterhead, son of Robert Keith, educated at Marischal College in Aberdeen, emigrated to America in 1720, minister in Henrico County, and Hamilton parish, Fauquier County, Virginia, died there in 1758. [VMHB.31.327][CCVC.29][EMA.38]

KEITH, JAMES FRANCIS EDWARD, born at Inverugie in 1696, a Jacobite exiled in 1716, served in the Russian army, later in the service of Frederick the Great of Prussia, was killed at the Battle of Hochkirchen on 14 October 1758. [Peterhead Monument]

KEITH, JOHN, son of Alexander Keith of Camculter, Rathen, and his wife Margaret Fraser, settled in Danzig around 1658, and was granted a birth brief by Aberdeen Town Council on 5 June 1672. [APB]

KEITH, JOHN, Episcopalian priest of Old Deer from 1710 to 1711. [SEC.532]

KEITH, JOHN, in Peterhead, in 1741, reference in deed. [NRS.GD67.173]

KEITH, JOHN, a ship's carpenter in Fraserburgh, married Susan Rennie in Fraserburgh on 15 November 1788. [NRS.CH12.32.2]

KEITH, NATHANIEL, of Cocklaw, in 1630. [VRA.206]

KEITH, ROBERT, graduated MA from St Andrews in 1645, minister at Old Deer from 1649 until 1663, husband of Euphemia Kinnear, parents of Jean Keith. [F.6.216]

KEITH, WILLIAM, of Ludquharn 1625, married Margaret Bannerman of Elsick, was created a Baronet of Nova Scotia, died 1666. [VRA.205]

KEITH, WILLIAM, the Earl Marischal, was served heir to his father in the Fishertoun of Peterhead with its harbour and anchorages, on 10 October 1637. [NRS.Retours. Aberdeen. 240]

KEMPT, THOMAS and KATHERINE, children of Alexander Kempt, a burgess of Aberdeen, and his wife Christine Jack, were granted land in the parish of Peterhead by King Charles I on 8 August 1635. [RGS.IX.396]

KENNEDY, ALEXANDER, a skipper in Fraserburgh, testament, 9 August 1771, Comm. Aberdeen. [NRS]

KERR, JOHN, master of the Star of Peterhead from Prestonpans to Virginia in 1668. [NRS.AC7.4]

KERR, JOHN, husband of Isobel Anderson, in Peterhead, a sergeant of the Aberdeenshire Militia in 1804. [ACA.AS.AMI.6.1.1]

KILGOUR, ROBERT, born at Waulkmill, Cruden, in 1714, graduated from Aberdeen University in 1733, ordained in 1737, minister of St Peter's in Peterhead from 1737 to 1789, Bishop of Aberdeen in 1768, Bishop of Edinburgh and Primus of the Episcopal Church in 1782, consecrated Bishop Seabury, died 22 March 1790, husband of Margaret Arbuthnott. [SEC][TBD.223][Peterhead gravestone]

KILGOUR, THOMAS and ROBERT, woollen cloth manufacturers at Kinmundie, parish of Longside, 1790s. [OSA]

KING, WILLIAM, steersman of the Robert of Peterhead whaling off Greenland or the Davis Straits in 1791. [NRS.E508.91.8]

KINTRAE, JOHN, and his wife Margaret Taylor, in Pitsligo, testament, 20 July 1756, Comm. Aberdeen. [NRS]

KNOX, JOHN, a merchant in Gardenstown, husband of Mary Johnston, born 1760, died 22 March 1824. [New Deer gravestone]

LAMB, JOHN, in Pitblae, and Jean Massie, daughter of William Massie at Berry Mill, Rathen, were married in Fraserburgh on 29 October 1796. [NRS.CH12.32.2]

LAMB, ROBERT, mate of the Robert of Peterhead whaling off Greenland or the Davis Straits in 1791. [NRS.E508.91.8]

THE PEOPLE OF BUCHAN, 1600-1799

LARGOE, GEORGE, minister at Rathen, testament, 1 October 1771, Comm. Aberdeen. [NRS]

LARGOE, MARGARET, in Fraserburgh, widow of William Watson late farmer in Whitehall, Tyrie, testament, 3 December 1789, Comm. Aberdeen. [NRS]

LAW, GEORGE, born 1705 in Crimond, an Episcopalian minister and chaplain to Stonywood's regiment at Culloden in 1746. [JNES.31]

LAW, WILLIAM, schoolmaster of Strichen in 1679, later Episcopal minister at Slains, a Jacobite in 1715, deposed in 1717 [JNES.27][F.6.213]

LAWRENCE, JOHN, born at Skillimarno, Old Deer, on 25 June 1701, eldest son of Robert Lawrence and his wife Elspet May, a merchant in Old Deer, a Jacobite in 1745. [JAB]

LAURENCES, JOHN, line manager aboard the whaling ship Robert of Peterhead off Greenland and the Davis Straits in 1794. [NRS.E508.94.8.10]

LEASK, ALEXANDER, son of Gilbert Leask of Cruden, master of the Hart trading between Leith and Aberdeen in 1612. [ASW.73]

LEASK, MAGNUS, so of John Leask in Crimondgate and his wife Margaret Ferguson, died in Poland in 1585. [APB]

LEILL, JAMES, husband of Christine Pirie, in Pitsligo, married in Fraserburgh on 22 May 1803, a member of the Aberdeenshire Militia in 1806. [ACA.AS.AMI.6.1.1] [Fraserburgh Episcopal records]

LEITH, ELIZABETH, spouse of James Stewart in Fraserburgh, testament, 21 June 1804, Comm. Aberdeen. [NRS]

LESLIE, ELIZABETH, widow of William Cumine minister at Rathen, testament, 12 May 1803, Comm. Aberdeen. [NRS]

THE PEOPLE OF BUCHAN, 1600-1799

LESLIE, JAMES, MA, minister at Crimond fom 1709 until 1729. [F.6.213]

LESLIE, JOHN, in Easthill of Crimond, a charter, 21 May 1627. [NRS.GD124.1.321]

LESLIE, JOHN, in Tillymadein, Cruden, testament, 18 December 1753, Comm. Aberdeen. [NRS]

LESLIE, WILLIAM, a merchant in Old Aberdeen, supercargo aboard the Isobel of Fraserburgh bound from the Hermans Islands off Norway was captured by a French privateer in 1708. [ACA.APB.2]

LEYS, JOHN, a merchant in Peterhead, testament, 8 April 1736, Comm. Aberdeen. [NRS]

LILLY, JAMES, a skipper in Peterhead, a sasine, 1787. [NRS.RS.Aberdeen.652]

LILLIE, WILLIAM, in Kirkton of St Fergus, testament, 21 November 1792, Comm. Aberdeen, [NRS]

LIND, ALEXANDER, in Seatoun of Cairnbulg, testament, 23 December 1743, Comm. Aberdeen. [NRS]

LINDSAY, JOHN, bailie of Fraserburgh, testament, 29 April 1742, Comm. Aberdeen. [NRS]

LISK, JAMES, line manager aboard the whaling ship Robert of Peterhead off Greenland and the Davis Straits in 1794. [NRS.E508.94.8.10]

LISK, WILLIAM, line manager aboard the whaling ship Robert of Peterhead off Greenland and the Davis Straits in 1794. [NRS.E508.94.8.10]

LIVIE, WILLIAM, born 1792, a seaman from Fraserburgh, aboard the whaling ship the Oscar of Aberdeen bound for Greenland, was shipwrecked and drowned off Aberdeen on 1 April 1813. [Nigg grave]

LIVINGSTONE, CHRISTIAN, relict of Captain William Whyte a shipmaster in Peterhead, testament, 5 February 1807, Comm. Aberdeen. [NRS]

LIVINGSTONE, WILLIAM, Episcopalian priest of Old Deer from 1711 to his death in 1751, a Jacobite in 1715, died 1751. [SEC.532][JNES.28]

LOGAN, JOHN, a Jacobite in Fraserburgh in 1715. [JNES.28]

LORIMER, WILLIAM, a farmer in Ironhill, Pitsligo, a Jacobite in 1745. [JNES.33]

LOW, ALEXANDER, a seaman in Peterhead, a deed, 1693, [NRS.RD2.77.177]; in 1696, [PPA.1]

LOW, ALEXANDER, a merchant and skipper in Fraserburgh, testament, 15 November 1759, Comm. Aberdeen. [NRS]

LOW, GEORGE, a slater, and Mary Milne, both in Fraserburgh, married there on 4 August 1799. [NRS.CH12.32.2]

LOW, JAMES, born 1727, a squarewright in Fraserburgh, died 2 June 1814, husband of Ann Beattie, born 1732, died 1825, their son John Low, born 1776, a ship-carpenter, died 15 August 1844. [Fraserburgh Kirkton gravestone]

LOW, JOHN, born 1707, in West Kinglasser, died 20 September 1780. [Fraserburgh Kirkton gravestone]

LUMSDEN, JOHN, minister of Longside, 29 September 1722. [NRS.E647.75]

LUNDIE, JAMES or THOMAS, from Buchan, was educated at King's College, Aberdeen, a minister sent to Virginia in 1767. [EMA.41][FPA.309/330].

THE PEOPLE OF BUCHAN, 1600-1799

LUNDIE, JOHN, minister at Lonmay, 1790s. [OSA]

MCBEATH, ALEXANDER, a sailor of the Robert of Peterhead whaling off Greenland or the Davis Straits in 1791. [NRS.E508.91.8]

MACDONALD, BARBARA, in Fraserburgh, and Alexander Dalnoon, a weaver and widower from New Pitsligo, were married in Fraserburgh on 28 March 1799. [Fraserburgh Episcopal records]

MCDONALD, GEORGE, born 1786, a landsman from Peterhead, aboard the whaling ship the Oscar of Aberdeen bound for Greenland, was shipwrecked and drowned off Aberdeen on 1 April 1813. [Nigg grave]

MCDONALD, WILLIAM, husband of Margaret Dalziel, in Strichen, a member of the Aberdeenshire Militia in 1808. [ACA.AS.AMI.6.1.1]

MCINTOSH, HUGH, husband of Elizabeth Geddes, in Rathen, an army reservist in 1803. [ACA.AS.AMI.6.1.1]

MACKAY, WILLIAM, a chapman in Fraserburgh, testament, 13 December 1790, Comm. Aberdeen. [NRS]

MCKEAN, ROBERT, a seaman in Fraserburgh, a deed, 1693. [NRS.RD4.72.83]

MACKENZIE, KENNETH, in Blackwater of St Fergus, testament, 16 August 1748, Comm. Aberdeen. [NRS]

MACKENZIE, MARY, sometime in Park, Lonmay, testament, 1798. Comm. Aberdeen. [NRS]

MACKIE, ALEXANDER, born 1767 in Peterhead, a crewman of the herring buss Polly of Peterhead in 1792. [NRS.E508.94.9.56]

MACKIE, ALEXANDER, steersman aboard the ship Robert of Peterhead off Greenland in 1794. [NRS.E504.94.8/10]

MACKIE, ALEXANDER, a watchmaker in Peterhead, inventory, 3 July 1807, Comm. Aberdeen. [NRS]

THE PEOPLE OF BUCHAN, 1600-1799

MACKIE, ALEXANDER, in Hattonslap, then in Corbshill, New Deer, inventory, 27 April 1820, Comm. Aberdeen

MCKIE, GEORGE, born 1668 in Peterhead, a seaman enrolled into the king's service on 18 April 1690. [RPCS.XV.645]

MACKIE, GEORGE, a skipper in Colliston, Slains, in Fraserburgh 1696. [PPA.2]

MACKIE, JAMES, and Rachel Muirison, late servants in Tirrehill, Fraseburgh, married on 27 December 1806. [NRS.CH12.32.2]

MACKIE, JOHN, apprentice to John Farquharson of Crimond, successfully appealed against military impressment in 1757. [ACA.as.amil.2.17]

MACKIE, JOHN, line manager of the Robert of Peterhead whaling off Greenland or the Davis Straits in 1791. [NRS.E508.91.8]

MACKIE, MARGARET, in Gardenstoun, inventory, 9 August 1811, Comm. Aberdeen. [NRS]

MACKIE, THOMAS, a skipper in Aberdour, a deed, 1751. [NRS.RD3.211/1.586]

MACKIE, THOMAS, in the Kirkton of New Deer, testament, 24 July 1753, Comm. Aberdeen. [NRS]

MACKIE, WILLIAM, in the Lowden of Crimond, inventory, 21 May 1805, Comm. Aberdeen. [NRS]

MCKISSEN, JAMES, husband of Henrietta Birnie, in Fraserburgh, a member of the Aberdeenshire Militia in 1808. [ACA.AS.AMI.6.1.1]

MCLEA, WILLIAM, [Willem Mocklew], from Fraserburgh, was admitted as a citizen of Rotterdam in 1740. [GAR]

MCLEOD, ALEXANDER, formerly in the Service of the East India Company, later in Fraserburgh, testament, 19 November 1793, Comm. Aberdeen. [NRS]

THE PEOPLE OF BUCHAN, 1600-1799

MCLEOD, WILLIAM, from Fraserburgh, was admitted as a citizen of Rotterdam on 13 September 1740. [GAR]

MCPHEE, NEIL, husband of Christine Smith, in Peterhead, a member of the Aberdeenshire Militia in 1808. [ACA.AS.AMI.6.1.1]

MCPHERSON, GEORGE, master of the Peter of Peterhead, trading between Leith and Aberdeen in 1613. [ASW.78]

MCQUEEN, WILLIAM, husband of Margaret Cheyne, in Peterhead, a member of the Aberdeenshire Militia in 1808. [ACA.AS.AMI.6.1.1]

MAIR, DAVID, master of the Peter of Peterhead in Aberdeen in 1596. [ASW.25]

MAIR, GEORGE, born 1699, son of Reverend George Mair, minister at New Deer from 1722 until his death on 13 April 1736, husband of Margaret Lindsay, parents of Reverend William Mair. [F.6.219]

MAIR, MARGARET, born 1719, died 4 April 1810, her son John Mitchell sailed round the world under Commodore John Byron in 1764-1766. [New Deer gravestone]

MAITLAND, Baron ALEXANDER, was granted the lands of Strichen on 12 February 1711. [NRS.SIG1.113.41]

MAITLAND, ELIZABETH, in Fraserburgh, testament, 14 February 1740, Comm. Aberdeen. [NRS]

MAN, JAMES, at the Mill of Aden, testament, 15 January 1734, Comm. Aberdeen. [NRS]

MAR, GEORGE, husband of Bathia Burnet, in Fraserburgh, a member of the Aberdeenshire Militia in 1808. [ACA.AS.AMI.6.1.1]

MARR, HENDRY, son of William Marr in Peterhead, was apprenticed to Alexander Charles a wright in Aberdeen for 4 years, in May 1668. [ACA]

THE PEOPLE OF BUCHAN, 1600-1799

MARR, PETER, in Stuartfield, inventory, 3 May 1804, Comm. Aberdeen. [NRS]

MARTIN, ALEXANDER, brother of Reverend James Martin, minister at Old Deer by 1635, father of Major James Martin. [F.6.215]

MARTIN, JAMES, sr., minister at Peterhead from 1605 until 1623, husband of Isabel Arbuthnott. [F.6.231]

MARTIN, JAMES, jr., of Clerkhills, minister at Peterhead from 1636 to 1649, husband of Elizabeth daughter of John Arbuthnott of Carnegie, parents of Alexander and Nathaniel. [F.6.231][VRA.207]

MARTIN, NATHANIEL, was educated at Marischal College, Aberdeen, minister at Aberdour from 1646 until 1650, minister at Peterhead from 1650 to 1662, died in 1670s, husband of Jean Forbes. [F.6.209/231]; Nathaniel Martin, minister in Peterhead, and his wife Jean Forbes, a sasine, 1663. [NRS.GD33.10.22], a charter, 1663, [NRS.GD33.10.21]

MARTIN, ROBERT, of Clerkhill in 1662, later of Bruntbrae, deceased by 1669, husband of Jean Colville, parents of Nathaniel and Grizel. [VRA.207]

MASON, THOMAS, in Bilbao of Crimond, inventory, 7 March 1805, Comm. Aberdeen. [NRS]

MASSIE, WILLIAM, at Berry Mill, and Margaret Cruden, were married in Fraserburgh on 7 June 1800. [NRS.CH12.32.2]

MATHERS, ANDREW, born 1730, in South Culsh, died in May 1794, husband of Barbara Duncan, born 1723, died in May 1769, parents of William Mathers. [New Deer gravestone]

MATHER, CUSBART, a harpooner aboard the whaling ship Robert of Peterhead off Greenland in 1794. [NRS.E508.94.8/10]

THE PEOPLE OF BUCHAN, 1600-1799

MATTHEW, JEAN, in Peterhead, testament, 6 March 1811, Comm. Aberdeen. [NRS]

MATTHEW, THOMAS, a tailor in Fraserburgh, and Marjory Fraser, were married there on 31 December 1791. [NRS.CH12.32.2]

MAY, WILLIAM, a whitefisher in Cairnbulg, Rathen, in 1696. [PPA.1]

MEARNS, MARY, in Longside, inventory, 18 February 1819, Comm. Aberdeen. [NRS]

MELDRUM, ANN, in the Mains of Aberdour, widow of ..... Wemyss there, testament, 19 March 1770. Comm. Aberdeen. [NRS]

MESS, JAMES, a merchant in Rora, Longside, inventory, 26 November 1816, Comm. Aberdeen. [NRS]

MERCER, HUGH, born 1725 in Aberdeen, son of Reverend William Mercer in Pitsligo, educated at Marischal College, Aberdeen, around 1744, a physician and a Jacobite, to Philadelphia in 1746, settled in Franklin County, Pennsylvania, was a General of the American Army, fought at the Battles of Trenton and Princeton, died on 12 January 1777. [AP.278]

MERCER, JOHN, minister at Slains, was admitted as a burgess of Aberdeen on 30 August 1631. [ABR]

MERCER, JOHN, born 4 January 1677, son of Thomas Mercer of Todlaw and Smithyburn, and his wife Isabel Smith, graduated MA from Marischal College, Aberdeen, in 1704, minister at Tyrie from 1710 until his death on 31 March 1761. Husband of Isobel Martin, parents of John, Elizabeth, Thomas, Isobel, Agnes. [F.6.245]

MERCER, JOHN, son of John Mercer in the Kirkton of Tyrie, was apprenticed to William Murray a merchant in Aberdeen, for 5 years, 3 May 1774. [ACA]

MERCER, ROBERT, son of John Mercer minister at Slains, was admitted as a burgess of Aberdeen on 30 August 1631. [ABR]

THE PEOPLE OF BUCHAN, 1600-1799

MERCER, WILLIAM, minister at Pitsligo in 1729.
[NRS.CS271.517.13]

MIDDLETON, ALEXANDER, of Crimondgate, a merchant in
Aberdeen, testament, 20 November 1789, Comm. Aberdeen.
[NRS]

MIDDLETON, GEORGE, master of the James of Fraserburgh in
1690. [NRS.E72.1.18]

MIDDLETON, JAMES, a skipper in Fraserburgh, husband of
Margaret Boswell, a deed, 1696, [NRS.RD4.78.281]; a mariner in
Fraserburgh in 1696. [PPA.2]

MIDDLETON, JOHN, skipper of the Good Hope of Fraserburgh,
trading between Norway and Aberdeen, 1669, 1683,
[NRS.E72.1.1/9][ASW.572]; master of the Hope of Fraserburgh
trading between Inverness and Holland in 1685. [NRS.E72.11.11];
deeds, 1675, 1684, [NRS.RD4.36.848/RD3.68.729]; treasurer of
the Sea Box of Aberdeen, a deed, 1714. [NRS.RD4.114.43]

MIDDLETON, ROBERT, a porter in Fraserburgh, a Jacobite in 1745.
[JNES.38]

MIDDLETON, WILLIAM, a farmer in Techmuiry, inventory, 3
December 1821, Comm. Aberdeen. [NRS]

MILL, JOHN, son of Andrew Mill and his wife Janet Ligertwood in
Meikle Creich, Deer, a traveller in Poland, in 1601. [MSC.II.58]

MILL, JOHN, a labourer in Longside, a Jacobite in 1745,
imprisoned in Chester. [JNES.39]

MILL, WILLIAM, son of Andrew Mill and his wife Janet Ligertwood
in Meikle Creich, Deer, a traveller in Poland, in 1601. [MSC.II.58]

MILLER, SIMON, harpooner of the Robert of Peterhead whaling
off Greenland or the Davis Straits in 1791. [NRS.E508.91.8]

THE PEOPLE OF BUCHAN, 1600-1799

MILNE, ALEXANDER, born 1712, farmer in Quarryburn, died 16 March 1778, husband of Ann Morison, born 1722, died 15 November 1801. [Aberdour gravestone]

MILNE, ANNE, in Rosehearty, wido of Alexander Ingram in Stonebrigs, inventory, 20 February 1813, Comm. Aberdeen, [NRS]

MILNE, ANDREW, a seaman in Peterhead, in 1696. [PPA.1]

MILNE, ISABEL, in Middle Savock, Lonmay, testament, 12 July 1790, Comm. Aberdeen. [NRS]

MILNE, JAMES, born 1670 in Peterhead, a seaman who was enrolled into the king's service in 1690. [RPCS.XV.645]

MILNE, JAMES, husband of Helen Deans, in New Pitsligo, a member of the Aberdeenshire Militia in 1808. [ACA.AS.AMI.6.1.1]

MILNE, JAMES, a merchant in Rosehearty, testament, 31 May 1814, Comm. Aberdeen. [NRS]

MILNE, JEAN, widow of Thomas Ranson a skipper in Peterhead, testament, 15 November 1805, Comm. Aberdeen. [NRS]

MILNE, JOHN, a skipper in Peterhead, was admitted as a burgess of Banff in 1770. [BBR]

MILNE, JOHN, a merchant in Peterhead, inventory, 21 August 1802, Comm. Aberdeen. [NRS]

MILNE, MARGARET, widow of Captain Pember Britton once a skipper in Aberdeen, now in Peterhead, testament, 25 November 1770, Comm. Aberdeen. [NRS]

MILNE, THOMAS, born 1764, minister at Peterhead [Antiburgher] Church from 1796 to 1815, died in Dunfermline on 15 January 1835. [UPC.140]

MILNE, WILLIAM, born 1668 in Peterhead, a seaman who was enrolled into the king's service in 1690. [RPCS.XV.645]

THE PEOPLE OF BUCHAN, 1600-1799

MILNE, WILLIAM, a merchant in Seaton of Cairnbulg, testament, 18 April 1777, Comm. Aberdeen. [NRS]

MILNE, WILLIAM, a merchant in Rosehearty, Pitsligo, inventory, 29 August 1815, Comm. Aberdeen. [NRS]

MINTO, Captain J., master of the Jean of Peterhead, from Peterhead on 19 March 1826 bound for Greenland, on 18 April the ship was wrecked and the crew landed on Grimsay off Iceland, of the 51 man crew at least 6 died, the survivors returned to Peterhead in August 1826. [AJ]

MITCHELL, ALEXANDER, a skipper in Fraserburgh, a deed, 1665. [NRS.RD3.11.108]

MITCHELL, ANDREW, in the Barnyards of St Fergus, executry papers, 1743 to 1749. [NRS.CC1.12.3]

MITCHELL, ANDREW, at Hallmoss, Inverallochy, inventory, 6 March 1817, Comm. Aberdeen. [NRS]

MITCHELL, or WEST, ANNE, servant to William Downie a white fisher in Seatoun of Pittullie, Pitsligo, accused of housebreaking and fire-raising – an outlaw and fugitive, 1800. [NRS.JC26.1800.56]

MITCHELL, GEORGE, in Fraserburgh, letters, 1766-1768. [NRS.RH9.4.117; RH15.27.105]; a merchant in Fraserburgh, testament, 8 January 1790, an inventory, 26 May 1808, Comm. Aberdeen. [NRS]

MITCHELL, JAMES, husband of Isabella Murray, in Peterhead, a member of the Aberdeenshire Militia in 1808. [ACA.AS.AMI.6.1.1]

MITCHELL, JANET, died 3 June 1746. [Crimond gravestone]

MITCHELL, JEAN, in Fraserburgh, married William Chalmers from New Deer, in Fraserburgh on 10 July 1790. [Fraserburgh Episcopal records]

THE PEOPLE OF BUCHAN, 1600-1799

MITCHELL, JOHN, in Peterhead, was served heir to his great-grandfather George Brook in Myreside, on 3 October 1766. [NRS.S/H]

MITCHELL, JOHN, son of Robert Mitchell in Balmoor near Peterhead, was apprenticed to John Tower a cooper in Aberdeen for 5 years, 20 May 1773. Cautioner was James Arbuthnot a merchant in Peterhead. [ACA]

MITCHELL, MARGARET, in Kirktoun of St Fergus, widow of Wiliam Steven in Blackwater, testament, 20 April 1748, Comm. Aberdeen. [NRS]

MITCHELL, ROBERT, in Overtoun of Knaven, New Deer, inventory, 3 April 1823, Comm. Aberdeen. [NRS]

MITCHELL, THOMAS, bailie of Fraserburgh, a deed, 1693. [NRS.RD2.76.397]

MITCHELL, WILLIAM, a skipper in Fraserburgh, a deed, 1665. [NRS.RD3.11.109]

MITCHELL, WILLIAM, a merchant in Old Deer, testament, 30 November 1768, Comm. Aberdeen. [NRS]

MITCHELL, WILLIAM, born 1747, minister of Clola [Antiburgher] Church from 1770, died 16 April 1832. [UPC.135]

'MOCKLAW, WILLEM', from 'Fresisburg' [Fraserburgh?] was admitted as a citizen of Rotterdam on 13 September 1740. [GAR]

MOIR, GEORGE, master of the Charles of Peterhead trading between Aberdeen, Holland and Flanders, in 1612-1613. [ASW.73/75]

MOIR, GEORGE, born 5 April 1741, son of Andrew Moir minister at Ellon, was educated at Marischal College, Aberdeen, 1755 to 1759, minister at Peterhead from 1763 until his death on 18

THE PEOPLE OF BUCHAN, 1600-1799

March 1818, husband of Martha daughter of Patrick Byres of Tonley. [F.6.232]

MOIR, WILLIAM, of Invernetty, Peterhead, born 1669, a merchant in Aberdeen and a Jacobite in 1715, testament, 22 December 1744, Comm. Aberdeen. [NRS][JNES.31]

MOIR, WILLIAM, of Lonmay, eldest son of James Moir of Stonywood and his wife Jean Abernethy, a Jacobite in 1745. [JNES.40]

MOIR, WILLIAM, of Lonmay, a deed, 2 February 1768. [NRS.GD67.69]

MOIR, WILLIAM, land owner of Invernetty in the parish of Peterhead in 1770. [NRS.E106.36.5]

MONTGOMERIE, ROBERT, in the Mains of Crichie, inventory, 3 August 1816, Comm. Aberdeen. [NRS]

MOORE, ALEXANDER, Episcopalian priest of Fraserburgh from 1703 to 1717. [SEC]; son of Reverend James Moore, graduated MA from King's College, Aberdeen, in 1681, minister at Fraserburgh from 1703, died 20 April 1717. [F.6.222]

MOORE, JAMES, Episcopalian priest of Fraserburgh from 1667 to 1703. [SEC]; born 1631, educated at King's College, Aberdeen, minister at Fraserburgh from 1666 until his death on 23 March 1703, husband of Margaret Crawford, parents of Elizabeth, Margaret, Helen, Isobel, and Alexander. [F.6.222]

MORISON, ALEXANDER, a sailor in Fraserburgh, a Jacobite in 1745. [JNES.41]

MORISON, GEORGE, a vintner in New Deer, testament, 18 December 1776, Comm. Aberdeen. [NRS]

MORISON, THOMAS, a cooper in Fraserburgh, testament, 1799, Comm. Aberdeen. [NRS]

THE PEOPLE OF BUCHAN, 1600-1799

MOWAT, HELEN, wife of Nathaniel Craig factor of Pitsligo, testament, 7 June 1762, Comm. Aberdeen. [NRS]

MOUAT, WILLIAM, a whitefisher in Cairnbulg, Rathen, in 1696. [PPA.1]

MUIR, ANDREW, a mariner in Peterhead, a sasine in 1621. [NRS.RS.Aberdeen.4.3.155]

MUIR, JOHN, a skipper in Peterhead in 1656. [RGS.X.534]

MUIR, THOMAS, a skipper in Peterhead, husband of Catherine Body, in 1642. [ASC.3.2]

MUNRO, DONALD, a sailor aboard the whaling ship Robert of Peterhead off Greenland and the Davis Straits in 1794. [NRS.E508.94.8.10]

MUNRO, JOHN, husband of Jean Robertson, in Longside, a member of the Aberdeenshire Militia in 1808. [ACA.AS.AMI.6.1.1]

MURDO, WILLIAM, in Inverchumbrie, Longside, 22 August 1622. [ASC]

MURDOCH, JOHN, born 1742, died 20 June 1837, husband of Ann Tilleray, born 1742, died at Tillynauld on 5 March 1825. [Aberdour gravestone]

MURDOCH, NATHANIEL, in the Kirktoun of St Fergus, testament, 8 December 1739, Comm. Aberdeen. [NRS]

MURRAY, ALEXANDER, a seaman in Peterhead in 1696. [PPA.1]

MURRAY, GEORGE, a merchant in Old Deer, testament, 12 August 1751, Comm. Aberdeen. [NRS]

MURRAY, JAMES, a merchant in Fraserburgh, papers, 1741-1748. [NRS.GD164.347]; testament, 14 April 1760, Comm. Aberdeen. [NRS]

THE PEOPLE OF BUCHAN, 1600-1799

MURRAY, PATRICK, at Ardiffery of Cruden late in Peterhead, inventory, 6 August 1816, Comm. Aberdeen. [NRS]

MURRAY, WILLIAM, an apprentice of the Robert of Peterhead whaling off Greenland or the Davis Straits in 1791. [NRS.E508.91.8]

MUTCH, GEORGE, in New Deer, testament, 5 August 1789, Comm. Aberdeen. [NRS]

MUTCH, JAMES, in Ironside of New Deer, husband of Ann Gray, born 1742, died 1 March 1821, parents of Jean born 1776, died 26 May 1788, Robert born 1786, died 21 December 1791. [New Deer gravestone]

NEILLSON, JOSEPH, a harpooner aboard the whaling ship Robert of Peterhead off Greenland in 1794. [NRS.E508.94.8/10]

NICOLL, GEORGE, a whitefisher in Longhaven, Cruden, in 1696. [PPA.2]

NICOLL, JAMES, a skipper in Gardenston, inventory, 10 May 1805, Comm. Aberdeen. [NRS]

NICOL, WILLIAM, in Clerkhill, Peterhead, testament, 8 January 1767, Comm. Aberdeen. [NRS]

NICOLL, WILLIAM, a skipper in Gardenstown, later in Peterhead, inventory, 25 September 1812. [NRS.CC1.w541]

NICOLSON, GEORGE, and Jane Stephen, from Longside, were married in Fraserburgh on 1 March 1794. [NRS.CH12.32.2]

NIDDRAY, ALEXANDER, a weaver in Fraserburgh, a Jacobite in 1745. [JNES.42]

NIDDRIE, GEORGE, and Margaret Rennie, both in Fraserburgh, were married there on 8 January 1789. [NRS.CH12.32.2]

THE PEOPLE OF BUCHAN, 1600-1799

NIDDRY, JOHN, a carrier in Old Deer, testament, 23 April 1751, Comm. Aberdeen. [NRS]

NOBLE, ALEXANDER, born 1780, died 15 April 1829, brother of William Noble a merchant in Fraserburgh. [Fraserburgh Kirkton gravestone]

NOBLE, ANDREW, born 1707, a whitefisher in Broadsea, died 8 March 1784. [Fraserburgh gravestone]

NOBLE, GEORGE, a skipper in Peterhead, testament, 1768, Comm. Edinburgh. [NRS]

NOBLE, JAMES, a seaman in Fraserburgh in 1696. [PPA.2]

NOBLE, JOHN, a mariner in Fraserburgh, a deed, 1699. [NRS.RD4.85.620]

NORIE, ALEXANDER, a sailor aboard the whaling ship Robert of Peterhead off Greenland and the Davis Straits in 1794. [NRS.E508.94.8.10]

NORIE, ANDREW, a sailor aboard the whaling ship Robert of Peterhead off Greenland and the Davis Straits in 1794. [NRS.E508.94.8.10]

OGILVIE, ALEXANDER, of Auchiries, born 1723, died 1791, a landowner in the parish of Rathen in 1770. [NRS.E106.36.5]

OGILVIE, ALEXANDER, a merchant in Peterhead, testament, 3 January 1803, Comm. Aberdeen. [NRS]

OGILVIE, CHARLES, born 1731, son of James Ogilvie of Auchiries, a merchant in Charleston, South Carolina, in 1762 he married Mary, daughter of James Michie the Chief Justice there, later in London, a Loyalist in 1776, died 1788. [TNA.AO12.48.63, etc] [AUL.ms2740/10]

THE PEOPLE OF BUCHAN, 1600-1799

OGILVIE, GEORGE, born 1748, son of Alexander Ogilvie of Auchiries and his wife Mary Cumine, emigrated in 1774, via London to Charleston, South Carolina, a planter there, a Loyalist in 1776, returned to Scotland, married Rebecca Irvine, was appointed the Customs Controller, died in 1801. [AUL.ms2740][TNA.AO12.51.227, etc]

OGILVIE, JAMES, of Auchiries, husband of Margaret Strachan, 1715. [AUL.ms2740/10]

OGILVIE, JAMES, in Toux, testament, 15 May 1731, Comm. Aberdeen. [NRS]

OGILVIE, PATRICK, in Cairnbulg, 25 January 1703. [NRS.GD67.13]

OGILVIE, Colonel PATRICK, was granted the lands of Lonmay on 29 November 1714. [NRS.SIG1.129.38]

OGILVIE, THOMAS, a dyer in Fraserburgh, testament, 7 March 1755, Comm. Aberdeen. [NRS]

OGSTON, ALEXANDER, a tidewaiter in Fraserburgh, testament, 4 June 1781, Comm. Aberdeen. [NRS]

OGSTON, JAMES, a merchant in Peterhead, testament, 10 March 1729, Comm. Aberdeen. [NRS]

OGSTON, JAMES, born 1714, died 21 August 1789, husband of Jean Milne, born 1700, died 25 November 1798. [Aberdour gravestone]

OGSTON, ROBERT, bailie of Fraserburgh, a letter, 3 June 1619. [ACL.165]

OLIPHANT, ALEXANDER, in Old Maud, testament, 22 March 1771, Comm. Aberdeen. [NRS]

OLIPHANT, WILLIAM, and MARGARET MURRAY, were married in Fraserburgh on 13 August 1791. [NRS.CH12.32.2]

PANTON, JAMES, in Burnside of Strichan, testament, 12 January 1738, Comm. Aberdeen. [NRS]

PANTON, JOHN, born 1726, of the Mains of Aberdour, died18 August 1801, husband of Barbara Wemyss, born 1719, died 26 March 1780. [Aberdour gravestone]

PANTON, MARGARET, relict of Alexander Forbes of Pitsligo, a deed, 1693. [NRS.RD72.699/833]

PANTON, WALTER, a merchant in Fraserburgh, a deed, 1693. [NRS.RD2.76.13]

PARK, ANDREW, in Lonmay, husband of Elspeth Jaffrey, a sasine, 7 July 1613. [NRS.GD28.9]

PARK, ANDREW, a merchant in Peterhead, testament, 18 February 1755, Comm. Aberdeen. [NRS]

PARK, JAMES, born 1718, farmer in Little Byth, died 9 May 1754, son of Alexander Park. [Aberdour gravestone]; testament, 25 February 1755, Comm. Aberdeen. [NRS]

PARK, JAMES, master of the James of Peterhead, trading between Bumblefiord and Aberdeen in 1743. [NRS.E504.1.1]; a skipper in Fraserburgh in 1767, [AJ.1004]; born 1700, a skipper in Peterhead, died on 10 April 1772, husband of Grizel Arbuthnott, born 1701, died in 1790. [Peterhead gravestone]; a Jacobite in 1715. [JNES.32]

PARK, JAMES, born 1710, in Mossneuk of Longside, died 10 July 1775, his wife Mary Cullen, born 1727, died 5 February 1795, son William born 1762, died 9 July 1793. [Crimond gravestone]

PARK, JOHN, in the Hill of Crimond, testament, 30 May 1754, Comm. Aberdeen. [NRS]

PARK, WILLIAM, born 1676, farmer of Mains of Crimond, died 8 March 1763, wife Elizabeth Farquhar, born 1683, died 4 January

1757, son William, born 1716, farmer in Crimondgorth, died 2 February 1765, husband of Margaret Cruickshank. [Crimond gravestone]

PARK, WILLIAM, a tailor in Boddam, Peterhead, testament, 24 September 1813, Comm. Aberdeen. [NRS]

PARK, Misses, white thread manufacturers in Peterhead in 1764. [OSA]

PATERSON, GEORGE, in Peterhead, testament, 4 May 1805, Comm. Aberdeen. [NRS]

PATERSON, ISOBEL, in New Pitsligo, testament, 26 September 1818, Comm. Aberdeen. [NRS]

PATERSON, JANE, in Peterhead, widow of Joseph Johnston late quartermaster of the 1th Regiment of Foot, testament, 11 October 1779, Comm. Aberdeen. [NRS]

PATERSON, LEWIS, line manager of the Robert of Peterhead whaling off Greenland or the Davis Straits in 1791. [NRS.E508.91.8]

PATERSON, WILLIAM, minister of parish of Slains, 1790s. [OSA]

PATTOUN, ROGER, of Over Craigie in the parish of Longside, husband of Marjorie Smith, 1657. [VRA.208]

PEACOCK, WILLIAM, master of the Robert of Peterhead whaling off Greenland or the Davis Straits in 1791. [NRS.E508.91.8]; also, in 1794. [NRS.E508.94.8/10]

PEDDER, JANET, daughter of Thomas Pedder in Old Deer, testament, 22 July 1726, Comm. Aberdeen. [NRS]

PETRIE, JOHN, tenant in Stewartfield, born 1741, died 22 March 1825, husband of Elisabeth Anderson, born 1749, died 8 May 1825. [New Deer gravestone]

THE PEOPLE OF BUCHAN, 1600-1799

PIRIE, GEORGE, a periwig-maker in Fraserburgh, a Jacobite in 1715. [JNES.33]

PIRIE, JAMES, in Fraserburgh, a member of the Aberdeenshire Militia in 1803. [ACA.AS.AMI.6.1.1]

PITTENDREACH, JAMES, a farmer in the Kirkton of Tyrie, Pitsligo, and Sophia Ramsay, alias Mrs Lachlan Milne, in Pitsligo, were married in Fraserburgh on 26 September 1795. [NRS.CH12.32.2]

PETTINDREICH, JOHN, a notary public in Fraserburgh, a charter witness on 25 August 1624. [RGS.VIII.777]

PITTENDREICH, MARY, in Nether Kinmundy, Longside, daughter of James Pittendreich a gardener in Longside, testament, 21 May 1793, Comm. Aberdeen. [NRS]

PHILIP, ALEXANDER, [1], a whitefisher in Finniefold, Cruden, in 1696. [PPA.2]

PHILIP, ALEXANDER, [2], a whitefisher in Wardhill, Cruden, in 1696. [PPA.2]

PHILIP, ALEXANDER, [3], a whitefisher in Longhaven, Cruden, in 1696. [PPA.2]

PHILIP, GEORGE, a whitefisher in Finniefold, Cruden, in 1696. [PPA.2]

PHILIP, GEORGE, a whitefisher in Wardhill, Cruden, in 1696. [PPA.2]

PHILIP, GEORGE, a skipper in Colliston, Slains, in 1696. [PPA.2]

PHILIPS, JAMES, schoolmaster at Cruden, 1723-1725. [NRS.CH1.2.48.47-86]

PHILIP, JOHN, a whitefisher in Finniefold, Cruden, in 1696. [PPA.2]

THE PEOPLE OF BUCHAN, 1600-1799

PHILIP, THOMAS, a whitefisher in Finniefold, Cruden, in 1696. [PPA.2]

PHILIP, WILLIAM, a whitefisher in Finniefold, Cruden, in 1696. [PPA.2]

PHILIP, WILLIAM, the younger, a whitefisher in Finniefold, Cruden, in 1696. [PPA.2]

PHILP, ALEXANDER, a sailor of the Robert of Peterhead whaling off Greenland or the Davis Straits in 1791. [NRS.E508.91.8]

PHINNIE, ANDREW, eldest son of Andrew Phinnie a bailie of Peterhead deceased, 1656. [RGS.X.535]

PIRIE, JOHN, a sailor of the Robert of Peterhead whaling off Greenland or the Davis Straits in 1791. [NRS.E508.91.8]

PIRIE, WILLIAM, born 1613, schoolmaster at Aberdour, died 29 April 1683, father of George Pirie farmer at the Mains of Aberdour, born 1662, died 17 April 1748, husband of Elizabeth Bruce, born 1665, died 2 September 1745, parents of Barbara, Magdalene, Margaret, and Ann. [Aberdour gravestone]

PRESLEY, CHARLES, a merchant in Fraserburgh, and Margaret Moir from Lonmay, were married in Fraserburgh on 15 July 1798. [NRS.CH12.32.2]

PRESLEY, JAMES, a weaver in Fraserburgh, a widower, and Isobel Cardno, a widow, were married in Fraserburgh on 14 June 1794. [NRS.CH12.32.2]

PRESLEY, JOHN, a shoemaker in Fraserburgh, and Jean Sinclair, were married in Fraserburgh on 13 September 1788. [NRS.CH12.32.2]

PRYSE, ALEXANDER, from Rathen, was granted a birth brief by Aberdeen Town Council on 3 June 1648. [APB.I]

THE PEOPLE OF BUCHAN, 1600-1799

PROTT, GEORGE, in Fraserburgh, a charter witness on 25 August 1624. [RGS.VIII.777]

PROTT, WILLIAM, a mariner in Fraserburgh in 1696. [PPA.2]

PYPER, GEORGE, from Fraserburgh, and Margareta Anderson from Rotterdam, were married in Rotterdam on 12 December 1713. [GAR]; he was admitted as a citizen of Rotterdam on 4 October 1715. [GAR]

QUEE, JOHN, a mariner from Tilliemont, Tyre, died aboard the George, probate, 1678, PCC. [TNA]

RAINIE, ALEXANDER, servant to William Cruickshank a tanner at Backhill of Old Deer, successfully appealed against military impressment in 1757. [ACA.as.amil.2.17]

RAINY, JOHN, a sailor in Fraserburgh in 1777. [NRS.S/H]

RAINY, JOHN, a merchant later post in Fraserburgh, testament, 16 May 1778. [NRS]

RAMSAY, ALEXANDER, a skipper in Fraserburgh, documents, 1679, [NRS.GD305.1.147.53]; deeds, 1681/1682. [NRS.RD3.53.392/RD2.56.258]

RAMSAY, ARTHUR, a merchant in Rosehearty, testament, 13 July 1743, Comm. Aberdeen. [NRS]

RAMSAY, JOHN, of Culsh, was served heir to his father Archibald Ramsay in property in Fraserburgh on 14 November 1627. [NRS.Retours.Aberdeen.204]

RAMSAY, JOHN, Major of the Peterhead Volunteers, 1799-1801. [NRS.GD44.47.45/4]

RAMSAY, WILLIAM, graduated MA from St Andrews in 1644, minister at Aberdour from 1651 to 1662, deprived in 1662, restored in 1690, died 31 December 1690. [F.6.209][Aberdour gravestone]

THE PEOPLE OF BUCHAN, 1600-1799

RAMSAY, WILLIAM, born 1683, a ship's carpenter, died 14 April 1754. [Fraserburgh gravestone]; a Jacobite in 1715. [JNES.33]

RANKIN, ARTHUR, from Aberdeen, married Sarah Funston, in Fraserburgh on 23 February 1797. [Fraserburgh Episcopal records]

RANKEN, WILLIAM, born 1769, a square-wright in Fraserburgh, died 31 January 1855, husband of Mary Watson, born 1773, died 16 February 1853. [Fraserburgh Kirkton gravestone]

RANKIN, WILLIAM, from Fraserburgh, died in New York on 22 June 1853. [AJ.20.7.1853]

REID, CHARLES, a skipper in Fraserburgh, testament, 1789, Comm. Aberdeen. [NRS][AJ.2144]

REID, GEORGE, mate of the Isobel of Fraserburgh bound from Rotterdam via Aberdeen to Bergen, Norway, in 1750. [SNS.107]

REID, JAMES, a skipper in Fraserburgh, owner of the sloop Jean and the sloop Lady Saltoun in 1789. [AJ.2139]; an inventory, 10 February 1808. [NRS.CC1.w343]; testament, 10 February 1808, Comm. Aberdeen. [NRS]

REID, JOHN, born 1679, tenant in Mill of Auchmeddan, died 31 May 1754, husband of Bathia Bartlet, born 1690, died 2 August 1753, parents of James, John, Ann, Sarah, Jean, Janet, and William. [Aberdour gravestone]

REID, JOHN, master of the Friendship of Peterhead trading between Aberdeen and Bergen in 1743; from Aberdeen to Arundale in 1743. [NRS.E504.1.1]; trading with Muldo, Arundale, Bergen, Christiansands, Oslo and Danzig, in 1749-1752, [NRS.E504.1.3/4]; in 1788. [AJ.2151]

REID, JOHN, a builder in Peterhead, ledger of a joiner's shop in Peterhead, 1817-1823. [NRS.CS238.Misc.23/11; CS235. R21.16]

THE PEOPLE OF BUCHAN, 1600-1799

REID, MARGARET, in Fraserburgh, testament, 6 August 1811, Comm. Aberdeen. [NRS]

REID, MARY, daughter of James Reid a shipmaster in Fraserburgh, married John J. J. Alexander from St Lucia, in Bath on 31 August 1813. [SM.75.798]

REID, ROBERT, a wright in Peterhead, a deed, 1693. [NRS.RD2.77.i.535]

REID, THOMAS, master in H M Navy Yard in Halifax, Nova Scotia, later in Peterhead, an inventory, 18 December 1804. [NRS.CC1.w205]; testament, 18 December 1804, Comm. Aberdeen. [NRS]

REID, WILLIAM, a merchant in New Deer, testament, 1790, Comm. Aberdeen. [NRS]

REID, WILLIAM, a skipper in Peterhead, testament, 1792, Comm. Aberdeen. [NRS]

RENNIE, ALEXANDER, husband of Margaret Martin, in Rora, Longside, a member of the Aberdeenshire Militia in 1808. [ACA.AS.AMI.6.1.1]

REYNOLD, ALEXANDER, son of Alexander Reynold a burgess of Montrose, educated at King's College, Aberdeen, minister at Aberdour from 1665 to 1690, died 9 August 1691. Husband of Margaret Forbes who died on 28 February 1695. [F.6.210] [Aberdour gravestone]

RICHART, WILLIAM, a seaman in Peterhead in 1696. [PPA.1]

RIND, WILLIAM, a seaman in Aberdour in 1696. [PPA.2]

RITCHIE, ALEXANDER, a fisherman in the service of Sir William Keith of Ludquharn, who absconded in 1683. [RPCS.VIII.119]

RITCHIE, ALEXANDER, [1], a seaman in Rosehearty, Pitsligo in 1696. [PPA.2]

THE PEOPLE OF BUCHAN, 1600-1799

RITCHIE, ALEXANDER, [2], a seaman in Rosehearty, Pitsligo in 1696. [PPA.2]

RITCHIE, ALEXANDER, [3], a seaman in Rosehearty, Pitsligo in 1696. [PPA.2]

RITCHIE, ANDREW, a skipper in Fraserburgh in 1611. [ASC.2.168]

RITCHIE, ANDREW, son of Patrick Ritchie in Peterhead, was apprenticed to Walter Cochrane a bailie of Aberdeen, on 12 January 1648, for 6 years. [ACA]

RITCHIE, ANDREW, a fisherman in the service of Sir William Keith of Ludquharn, who absconded in 1683. [RPCS.VIII.119]

RITCHIE, ANDREW, a skipper in Fraserburgh in 1696, [PPA.2]; a deed, 1699. [NRS.RD4.85.622]

RITCHIE, ANDREW, [1], a seaman in Rosehearty, Pitsligo, in 1696. [PPA.2]

RITCHIE, ANDREW, [2], a seaman in Rosehearty, Pitsligo, in 1696. [PPA.2]

RITCHIE, ANDREW, [3], a seaman in Rosehearty, Pitsligo, in 1696. [PPA.2]

RITCHIE, ANDREW, a skipper in Fraserburgh, master of the Two Brothers of Fraserburgh, trading with Ireland, Zealand, and Portugal in 1745-1746, [NRS.E504.1.1]; in 1752. [AJ.211]

RITCHIE, ELZABETH, relict of .... Robertson a merchant in Fraserburgh, testament, 13 May 1811, Comm. Aberdeen. [NRS]

RITCHIE, GEORGE, a seaman in Rosehearty, Pitsligo, in 1696. [PPA.2]

RITCHIE, GILBERT, a seaman in Rosehearty, Pitsligo, in 1696. [PPA.2]

THE PEOPLE OF BUCHAN, 1600-1799

RITCHIE, GILBERT, a fresh or green man on the Robert of Peterhead whaling off Greenland or the Davis Straits in 1791. [NRS.E508.91.8]

RITCHIE, JAMES, master of the Swan of Fraserburgh, trading between Norway and Fraserburgh in 1690. [NRS.E72.1.18]

RITCHIE, JAMES, [1], a seaman in Rosehearty, Pitsligo, in 1696. [PPA.2]

RITCHIE, JAMES, [2], a seaman in Rosehearty, Pitsligo, in 1696. [PPA.2]

RITCHIE, JAMES, [3], a seaman in Rosehearty, Pitsligo, in 1696. [PPA.2]

RITCHIE, JAMES, master of the Margaret of Rosehearty trading with Kirkcaldy in 1750. [NRS.E504.1.3]

RITCHIE, JEAN, widow of George Mitchell a skipper in Fraserburgh, testament, 20 September 1820, Cmm. Aberdeen. [NRS]

RITCHIE, JOHN, master of the John of Fraserburgh in 1656, [ASW.402]; master of the Janet of Fraserburgh, deeds, 1670, 1691, [NRS.RD4.26.395; RD2.76.397]; trading between Norway and Fraserburgh in 1690, [NRS.E72.1.18]; a mariner in Fraserburgh in 1696. [PPA.2]

RITCHIE, JOHN, a seaman in Peterhead in 1696. [PPA.2]

RITCHIE, JOHN, a skipper in Fraserburgh, treasurer of the Sea Box of Fraserburgh, a deed, 1700. [NRS.RD2.83.746]; husband of Sophia Wilson, a deed, 1714. [NRS.RD3.143.650]

RITCHIE, MARGARET, spouse of .... Reid in Fraserburgh, testament, 4 May 1811, Comm. Aberdeen. [NRS]

RITCHIE, PATRICK, in Peterhead, 8 March 1638. [ASC]

RITCHIE, ROBERT, a skipper in Colliston, Slains, in 1696. [PPA.2]

THE PEOPLE OF BUCHAN, 1600-1799

RITCHIE, SOPHIA, relict of John Fraser a skipper in Fraserburgh, testament, 2 May 1811, Comm. Aberdeen. [NRS]

RITCHIE, THOMAS, [1], a seaman in Rosehearty, Pitsligo, in 1696. [PPA.2]

RITCHIE, THOMAS, [2], a seaman in Rosehearty, Pitsligo, in 1696. [PPA.2]

RITCHIE, WILLIAM, [1], a seaman in Rosehearty, Pitsligo, in 1696. [PPA.2]

RITCHIE, WILLIAM, [2], a seaman in Rosehearty, Pitsligo, in 1696. [PPA.2]

RITCHIE, or SOPER, WILLIAM, a seaman in Rosehearty, Pitsligo, in 1696. [PPA.2]

RITCHIE, WILLIAM, a seaman in Fraserburgh, in 1696. [PPA.2]; master of the Phoenix of Fraserburgh, a deed, 1699. [NRS.RD3.90.540]; trading between Norway and Aberdeen in 1691. [NRS.E72.1.20]

RITCHIE, WILLIAM, master of the Bettridge of Rosehearty trading with Kirkcaldy in 1750. [NRS.E504.1.3]

RITCHIE, WILLIAM, a skipper from Fraserburgh, an assessor of the Scots Court at Veere, Zeeland, in 1739. [NRS.RH11.2]

RITCHIE, WILLIAM, master of the Two Brothers of Fraserburgh trading with Flekkefjord and Rotterdam in 1752-1753. [NRS.E504.1.4]

RITCHIE, ..., master of the Jean of Rosehearty trading between Leith and Aberdeen in 1754. [AJ.330]

ROBB, ALEXANDER, and Isabel Davie, both in Fraserburgh, were married there on 23 April 1789. [NRS.CH12.32.2]

THE PEOPLE OF BUCHAN, 1600-1799

ROBB, WILLIAM, in Crimond, and Rebecca Catto in Rathen, were married in Fraserburgh on 31 July 1794. [NRS.CH12.32.2]

ROBERTSON, ALEXANDER, Episcopalian priest of Longside from 1687 to 1727. [SEC.530]; letters, 1723, [NRS.CH12.12.11-12]; a Jacobite in 1715. [JAB]Aberdeen. [NRS]

ROBERTSON, ALEXANDER, minister at Longside, testament, 1764, Comm. Aberdeen. [NRS]

ROBERTSON, ALEXANDER, a merchant in Fraserburgh, testament, 1767, Comm. Aberdeen. [NRS]

ROBERTSON, ALEXANDER, a farmer in Park, Lonmay, testament, 21 June 1816, Comm. Aberdeen. [NRS]

ROBERTSON, GEORGE, a skipper in Colliston, Slains, in 1696. [PPA.2]

ROBERTSON, GILBERT, a skipper in Peterhead, testament, 1735, Comm. Aberdeen. [NRS]

ROBERTSON, JAMES, a Jacobite in Fraserburgh in 1715. [JNES.34]

ROBERTSON, JAMES, a merchant in Rosehearty, testament, 1794, Comm. Aberdeen. [NRS]

ROBERTSON, ALEXANDER, sr., a merchant in Fraserburgh, testament, 15 July 1756, Comm. Aberdeen. [NRS]

ROBERTSON, GEORGE, in Nether Lochhills of Crimond, testament, 10 February 1820, Comm. Aberdeen. [NRS]

ROBERTSON, GILBERT, a skipper in Peterhead, testament, 14 August 1735, Comm. Aberdeen. [NRS]

ROBERTSON, JAMES, a merchant in Rosehearty, testament, 13 February 1794, Comm. Aberdeen. [NRS]

ROBERTSON, JOHN, a merchant in Peterhead, testament, 13 April 1801, Comm. Aberdeen. [NRS]

THE PEOPLE OF BUCHAN, 1600-1799

ROBERTSON, NATHANIEL, in Rora, 30 November 1642. [ASC]

ROBERTSON, ROBERT, born 1760, died in Peterhead in 1832. [AJ.2.12.1832]

ROBERTSON, WILLIAM, son of Alexander Robertson in New Deer, was apprenticed to Andrew Watson a butcher in Aberdeen for 4 years on 15 January 1659. [ACA]

ROBERTSON, WILLIAM, Episcopalian priest of Longside from 1727 to 1742. [SEC.530][EV.357]

ROBERTSON, WILLIAM, born 1747 in Peterhead, master and co-owner of the herring buss Polly of Peterhead in 1792. [NRS.E508.94.9.56]

ROSE, Reverend JAMES, in Udny, sermons, 1712-1762. [NRS.CH12.16.139]

ROSS, ALEXANDER, Episcopalian priest of Rathen from 1666 to 1694. [SEC.533]

ROSS, ARCHIBALD, husband of Janet Crichton, in Peterhead, a member of the Aberdeenshire Militia in 1805. [ACA.AS.AMI.6.1.1]

ROSS, ARTHUR, minister at Old Deer from 1663 to 1664. [F.6.216]

ROSS, GEORGE, a steersman aboard the whaling ship Robert of Peterhead off Greenland in 1794. [NRS.E508.94.8/10]

ROSS, JOHN, master of the Clementina of Peterhead trading between Veere and Aberdeen in 1751. [NRS.E504.1.4]

ROSS, JOHN, line manager of the Robert of Peterhead whaling off Greenland or the Davis Straits in 1791. [NRS.E508.91.8]

ROTHNEY or FRASER, ANN, relict of James Rothney in Kirkton of Crimond, testament, 17 April 1806, Comm. Aberdeen. [NRS]

RUSSELL, WILLIAM, in New Pitsligo, testament, 22 October 1812, Comm. Aberdeen. [NRS]

THE PEOPLE OF BUCHAN, 1600-1799

SANDERSON, ANDREW, an Elder of Fraserburgh, a letter, 3 June 1619. [ACL.165]

SANGSTER, BASIL, husband of Christine Presley, in Peterhead, a member of the Aberdeenshire Militia in 1805. [ACA.AS.AMI.6.1.1]

SANGSTER, CHARLES, in Lonmay, a Jacobite in 1745, accidentally shot in March 1746, buried at Essil. [JNES.47]

SANGSTER, JAMES, born 1794, a seaman from Peterhead, aboard the whaling ship the Oscar of Aberdeen bound for Greenland, was shipwrecked and drowned off Aberdeen on 1 April 1813. [Nigg grave]

SANGSTER, JOHN, son of Andrew Sangster in Longside, was apprenticed to William Strachan a baker in Aberdeen, for 5 years, 19 June 1785. Cautioner was John Moir in the Kirkton of Longside. [ACA]

SANGSTER, PARICK, a skipper in Gardenstoun, master of the sloop Happy Return, testament, 19 April 1773, Comm. Aberdeen. [NRS]

SANGSTER, THOMAS, born 1794, a seaman from Fraserburgh, aboard the whaling ship the Oscar of Aberdeen bound for Greenland, was shipwrecked and drowned off Aberdeen on 1 April 1813. [Nigg grave]

SANGSTER, WILLIAM, a labourer at the Bullers of Buchan, parish of Cruden, a Jacobite in 1745. [JNES.47]

SANGSTER, WILLIAM, born 1745, Episcopalian priest of Lonmay from 1769 to 1826. [SEC.530]; a letter, 1 April 1790; died in Lonmay in 1825. [NRS.CH12.30.24][AJ.4.1.1826]

SARKINGS, WILLIAM, harpooner of the Robert of Peterhead whaling off Greenland or the Davis Straits in 1791. [NRS.E508.91.8]; the master's mate aboard the whaling ship Robert of Peterhead off Greenland and the Davis Straits in 1794. [NRS.E508.94.8.10]

THE PEOPLE OF BUCHAN, 1600-1799

SCORGIACK, GEORGE, blacksmith in Woodhead, died 21 July 1748, husband of Isobel Mathers. [Aberdour gravestone]

SCORGIE, JANET, in Fraserburgh, testament, 17 May 1796, Comm. Aberdeen. [NRS]

SCOTT, JAMES, born 1782, a physician, died in the Kirkton of Fraserburgh in 1831. [AJ.14.8.1832]

SCOTT, JOHN, in Fraserburgh, a charter witness on 25 August 1624. [RGS.VIII.777]

SCOTT, JOHN, an apprentice aboard the whaling ship Robert of Peterhead off Greenland and the Davis Straits in 1794. [NRS.E508.94.8.10]

SCOTT, WILLIAM, jr., a merchant in Peterhead, testament, 3 April 1812, Comm. Aberdeen. [NRS]

SCOTT, WILLIAM, merchant in Peterhead, testament, 6 February 1815, Comm. Aberdeen. [NRS]

SEATOUN, MARJORIE, in Peterhead, a letter, 1679. [NRS.RH15.37.26]

SELLAR, ROBERT, a fisherman in the service of Sir William Keith of Ludquharn, who absconded in 1683. [RPCS.VIII.119]

SHAND, JAMES, of Craigelly, a landowner in the parish of Rathen in 1770. [NRS.E106.36.5]

SHAND, WILLIAM, died 20 May 1712, husband of Anna Blackhall, died 20 February 1716. [Aberdour gravestone]

SHAND, WILLIAM, a merchant in Peterhead, testament, 20 July 1751, Comm. Aberdeen. [NRS]

SHAND, ..., the organist of the Scotch Episcopal chapel in Peterhead, also a music tacher there, 1690s, [OSA]

THE PEOPLE OF BUCHAN, 1600-1799

SHARP, Reverend JOHN, born 1754, died at the Manse of New Pitsligo in 1837. [AJ.20.7.1837]

SHEARER, HUGH, minister of Lonmay, testament, 23 July 1812, Comm. Aberdeen. [NRS]

SHIVAS, ANDREW, a vintner in Peterhead, testament, 19 March 1795, Comm. Aberdeen. [NRS]

SHIVAS, JOHN, a merchant in Peterhead, testament, 24 July 1819, Comm. Aberdeen. [NRS]

SHORT, GEORGE, a sailor of the Robert of Peterhead whaling off Greenland or the Davis Straits in 1791. [NRS.E508.91.8]

SHURIE, WILLIAM, a mariner in Peterhead, an inventory, 24 September 1818. [NRS.CCI.W866]; testament, 24 September 1818, Comm. Aberdeen. [NRS]; Eik, 31 October 1818, Comm. Aberdeen. [NRS]

SIBBALD, ARBRAHAM, minister at Old Deer from 1586 until around 1630, husband of [1] Margaret Buist, widow of Reverend Gilbert Chisholm, [2] Christian Blackburn. [F.6.215]

SIBBALD, DAVID, born 1651, graduated MA from King's College, Aberdeen, in 1668, minister at New Deer from 1682 until his death on 15 May 1706. Husband of Elizabeth ....., parents of Marjorie, Elizabeth, Catherine, and Christian. [F.6.219]

SIMM, ALEXANDER, master of the Margaret of Fraserburgh trading with Kirkcaldy in 1749. [NRS.E504.1.3]

SIM, ANDREW, in Scotsmill, Peterhead, 1791. [NRS.E326.9.15]

SIMS, ANDREW, sometime in Jamaica, died in Peterhead on 9 February 1803. [Peterhead gravestone]; testament, 19 February 1803, Comm. Aberdeen. [NRS]

THE PEOPLE OF BUCHAN, 1600-1799

SIM, CHARLES, born 1794, an apprentice from Cruden, aboard the whaling ship the Oscar of Aberdeen bound for Greenland, was shipwrecked and drowned off Aberdeen on 1 April 1813. [AJ]

SIM, JAMES, a fisher in Pittuly, Pitsligo, inventory, 31 July 1821. [NRS.CC1.w1049]; testament, 31 July 1821, Comm. Aberdeen. [NRS]

SIM, JOHN TAIT, born 1789, a cook from Cruden, aboard the whaling ship the Oscar of Aberdeen bound for Greenland, was shipwrecked and drowned off Aberdeen on 1 April 1813. [AJ]

SIM, WILLIAM, a seaman in Aberdour in 1696. [PPA.2]

SIM, WILLIAM, a tanner in Strathend of Cruden, testament, 29 March 1811, Comm. Aberdeen. [NRS]

SIMPSON, ALEXANDER, born 1740, graduated MA from Marischal College in 1763, minister in Fraserburgh from 1780 to his deth 21 July 1814, husband o Rachel Scroggs, parents of George, Alexander did in Jamaica in 1834, William, Simon died in Jamaica in 1825, and Eleanora, testament, 17 February 1815, Comm. Aberdeen. [NRS][OSA][F.6.222]

SIMPSON, JANET, widow of Andrew Smith a merchant in Peterhead, testament, 24 August 1739, Comm. Aberdeen. [NRS]

SIMPSON, JOSEPH, master of the Happy Janet of Fraserburgh which was wrecked off Fraserburgh when on a voyage from Holland to Bergen in November 1750. [AJ.152][SNS.107]

SIMPSON, JOSEPH, master of the Prince Charles of Fraserburgh trading between Aberdeen, Kirkcaldy, Veere, Newcastle and Fraserburgh in 1751 to 1752. [AJ.165/172/217/231] [NRS.E504.1.4]; master of the Happy Isobel of Fraserburgh trading between Rotterdam and Aberdeen in 1751-1752. [NRS.E504.1.4]

SIMPSON, PETER, born 1726, died in Aberdour on 31 December 1813, husband of Isabella, born 8 March 1766, died 17 April 1843. [Aberdour gravestone]

SIMPSON, WILLIAM, born 1721, sometime in Dundarg, died 17 April 1778, father born 1764, died 13 January 1781, son John born 1759. [Aberdour gravestone]

SIMPSON, WILLIAM, husband of Mary Strachan, in New Pitsligo, Tyrie parish, a member of the Aberdeenshire Militia in 1807. [ACA.AS.AMI.6.1.1]

SIMSON, WILLIAM, son of William Simson in Colliston, was apprenticed to Samuel Hunter a cooper in Aberdeen for 5 years, on 18 December 1649. [ACA]

SIMS, ANDREW, sometime in Jamaica, died in Peterhead on 9 February 1803. [Peterhead gravestone]; testament, 19 February 1803, Comm. Aberdeen. [NRS]

SKELTON, GEORGE, a ship-owner in Peterhead, testament, 25 July 1815, Comm. Aberdeen. [NRS]

SKELTON, JAMES, a skipper in Peterhead, sasines, 1784 and 1798. [NRS.RS.Aberdeen.349/755]

SKINNER, ALEXANDER, harpooner of the Robert of Peterhead whaling off Greenland or the Davis Straits in 1791. [NRS.E508.91.8]

SKINNER, JOHN, born 3 October 1721 in the parish of Birse, educated at Marischal College in Aberdeen, Episcopalian priest of Longside from 1742 to 1807, died 16 June 1807. He married Grisell Hunter, parents of James, Margaret, Grace, Elizabeth, John, Marianus, and Alexander, the last three children emigrated to America or the West Indies. [SEC.530]

SKINNER, ROBERT, mason in Lemless, Aberdour, testament, 20 December 1776, Comm. Aberdeen. [NRS]

THE PEOPLE OF BUCHAN, 1600-1799

SKLAIT, GILBERT, on the Hill of Crimond, testament, 4 June 1728, Comm. Aberdeen. [NRS]

SLIGO, WILLIAM, a farmer in Kinninmonth, later in Peterhead, testament, 13 April 1821, Comm. Aberdeen. [NRS]

SMART, JAMES, born 1687 in Dysart, later in Peterhead, a seaman aboard the Angelica bound for Virginia in 1707. [TNA.HCA.Vol.84]

SMITH, AGNES, relict of William Bisset a shoemaker in Peterhead, testament, 6 June 1801, Comm. Aberdeen. [NRS]

SMITH, ALEXANDER, in Rora, deceased, husband of Beatrix Ord, 30 November 1642. [ASC]

SMITH, ALEXANDER, born 1701, died 25 January 1773, husband of Sarah Mackie, born 1705, died 17 May 1777, in Bilboa, parents of William and Isabel. [Crimond gravestone]

SMITH, ALEXANDER, born 1735, a mason in Bilbao, died 11 August 1826, husband of Janet Black, born 1734, died 18 March 1813, parents of Robert Smith, born 1766, died 1 January 1834, and Mary Smith, born 1769. [Crimond gravestone]

SMITH, ALEXANDER, a merchant in Fraserburgh, a Jacobite in 1715. [JNES.36]

SMITH, ALEXANDER, a shoemaker in New Deer, testament, 11 May 1815, Comm. Aberdeen. [NRS]

SMITH, ANDREW, in Overside of St Fergus, testament, 23 March 1730, Comm. Aberdeen. [NRS]

SMITH, CHARLES, sometime in the Kirkton of Cruden, testament, 21 November 1755, Comm. Aberdeen. [NRS]

SMITH, GEORGE, a feuar in Fraserburgh, husband of Isabell Bissett, testament, 10 August 1734, Comm. Aberdeen. [NRS]

THE PEOPLE OF BUCHAN, 1600-1799

SMITH, GEORGE, a skipper from Fraserburgh, an assessor at the Scots Court at Veere, Zeeland, in 1735. [NRS.RH11.2]

SMITH, GEORGE, master of the Margaret of Fraserburgh trading between Aberdeen and Christiansands in 1743. [NRS.E504.1.1]; testament, 13 February 1770, Comm. Aberdeen. [NRS]

SMITH, JAMES, a skipper in Peterhead in 1634. [ASC.2.394]

SMITH, JAMES, in Overside of St Fergus, testament, 10 February 1732, Comm. Aberdeen. [NRS]

SMITH, JAMES, a labourer in Old Deer, a Jacobite in 1745. [JNES.49]

SMITH, JAMES, born 1741, a mason in Haddo, died 16 June 1812, husband of Elspet Bruce, born 1753, died 4 September 1845. [Crimond gravestone]

SMITH, JAMES, and Company, book-sellers in Peterhead, sederunt book, 1819-1820. [NRS.CS233.Seqn.S1/57]

SMITH, JANET, daughter of William Smith a bailie of Peterhead, testament, 7 February 1733, Comm. Aberdeen. [NRS]

SMITH, JOHN, a seaman in Fraserburgh in 1696. [PPA.2]

SMITH, JOHN, a labourer in Old Deer, a Jacobite in 1745. [JNES.49]

SMITH, JOHN, minister in Strichen, 1763-1766. [NRS.RH15.27.90]

SMITH, JOHN, born 1747, a schoolmaster, died in Peterhead in 1829. [AJ.10.10.1829]

SMITH, JOHN, a travelling merchant in Crimond, testament, 24 February 1816, Comm. Aberdeen. [NRS]

SMITH, ROBERT, in Fraserburgh, a Jacobite in 1715. [JNES.36]

SMITH, WILLIAM, a skipper in Fraserburgh, a deed, 1680. [NRS.RD3.47.340]

THE PEOPLE OF BUCHAN, 1600-1799

SMITH, WILLIAM, minister at Peterhead from 1716 to 1717.
[F.6.232]

SMITH, WILLIAM, a wright in Broadgait, Peterhead, a sasine.
[NRS.RH1.2.515]

SMITH, WILLIAM, a merchant in Fraserburgh, testament, 17 April
1809, Comm. Aberdeen. [NRS]

SMITH, ..., a schoolmaster in Peterhead, 1790s. [OSA]

SOMERVILLE, PETER, in the Royal Navy, husband of Christine
Cockburn in Fraserburgh in 1782. [NRS.S/H]

SOUTAR, ALEXANDER, master of the master of Ann of Peterhead
trading with Kirkcaldy in 1750, and of the Robert and Mary of
Peterhead trading between Aberdeen, Rotterdam, Bo'ness, and
Arundale in 1752-1753. [NRS.E504.1.3/4]

SOUTAR, ANDREW, an apprentice of the Robert of Peterhead
whaling off Greenland or the Davis Straits in 1791.
[NRS.E508.91.8]

SOUTAR, JAMES, master of the Ann of Peterhead trading
between Alloa and Aberdeen in 1752. [NRS.E504.1.4]

SOUTAR, JAMES, a merchant in Peterhead, testament, 1774,
Comm. Aberdeen. [NRS]

SOUTTAR, JOHN, a harpooner aboard the whaling ship Robert of
Peterhead off Greenland in 1794. [NRS.E508.94.8/10]

SOUTTAR, JOHN, line manager the whaling ship Robert of
Peterhead off Greenland and the Davis Straits in 1794.
[NRS.E508.94.8.10]

SOUTAR, ..., master of the Mary of Cruden trading between
Leith and Aberdeen in 1751. [AJ.191]

THE PEOPLE OF BUCHAN, 1600-1799

SOUTAR, JOHN, master of the Anne of Peterhead in 1766. [AJ.942]

SOUTAR, JOHN, a skipper in Peterhead, an inventory, 2 May 1807, [NRS.CC1,W318]; testament, 2 May 1802, Comm. Aberdeen. [NRS]

SOUTAR, JOHN, born 1778, mate aboard the Enterprise of Peterhead, a whaler, in 1805, master of the Active of Peterhead a whaler, 1810-1813, master of the whaler Resolution of Peterhead from 1813, died 1858. [PWT.44]

SOUTAR, PETER, a merchant in Peterhead, testament, 15 December 1774, Comm. Aberdeen. [NRS]

SOUTAR, ROBERT, steersman of the Robert of Peterhead whaling off Greenland or the Davis Straits in 1791. [NRS.E508.91.8]

SOUTAR, WILLIAM, a skipper in Peterhead, son of John Soutar a skipper in Peterhead, a sasine, 1796. [NRS.RS.Aberdeen.1609]

SOUTAR, WILLIAM, a skipper in Peterhead, son of John Soutar a skipper there, in 1796. [NRS.S/H]

SOUTAR, ..., master of the Lovely Katie of Peterhead, trading between Peterhead and Danzig in 1783. [AJ.1853]

SOUTAR, ..., master of the Molly of Peterhead at Stromness in 1787. [AJ.2078]

SPENCE, GEORGE, son of George Spence in Tyrie, was apprenticed to Gilbert Duff a cooper in Aberdeen, for 3 years, 1710. [ACA]

SPENCE, NICOL, in Cruden, a letter, 1721. [NRS.CH1.2.44.159]

SPRITTIMAN, ANDREW, a skipper in Peterhead, trading between Leith and Aberdeen in 1626, 1627, 1629, and 1630. [ASW.125/142/147/154/172]

THE PEOPLE OF BUCHAN, 1600-1799

SPRITTIMAN, THOMAS, master of the Star of Peterhead, a deed, 1667. [NRS.RD3.16.256]

STEILL, ANDREW, a seaman in Burghsea, testament, 3 September 1728, Comm. Aberdeen. [NRS]

STEPHEN, WILLIAM, a sailor surgeon aboard the whaling ship Robert of Peterhead off Greenland and the Davis Straits in 1794. [NRS.E508.94.8.10]

STEVEN, ANDREW, a whitefisher in Cairnbulg, Rathen, in 1696. [PPA.1]

STEVENS, ROBERT, of Broadland land owner of Rattray, parish of Crimond, 1770. [NRS.E106.36.5]

STEVENSON, DAVID, minister at Pitsligo, testament 22 March 1787, Comm. Aberdeen. [NRS]

STEWART, ALEXANDER, bailie of Fraserburgh, letter, 3 June 1619. [ACL.165]

STEWART, ALEXANDER, master of the Prince Charles of Fraserburgh trading between Rotterdam and Aberdeen in 1748, [NRS.E504.1.3]; master of the Pretty Peggy of Fraserburgh trading with Norway in 1750, [NRS.E504.1.3]; master of the Peggie of Fraserburgh trading between Aberdeen and Fraserburgh in 1751. [AJ.191]; from Fraserburgh to London in 1753. [AJ.278]; master of the Elenora of Fraserburgh from London to Peterhead, Fraserburgh, and Banff in 1766. [AJ.985]

STEWART, Captain Archibald, in Strichen, letters, 1767-1768. [NRS.RH15.27.117]

STEWART, JOHN, son of Walter Stewart of Bogton of Carnowsie, graduated MA from King's College, Aberdeen, in 1649, ordained in 1654, minister at Crimond from 1655 until 1660, deposed as a Covenanter, in 1685 he was banished and later confined on the Bass Rock until 1686. Husband of Christian Arbuthnot, parents of Mary and Elizabeth. [F.6.213]

THE PEOPLE OF BUCHAN, 1600-1799

STEWART, PETER, a tailor in Peterhead, testament, 28 May 1821, Comm. Aberdeen. [NRS]

STEWART, ..., master of the Nelly and Peggy of Fraserburgh was captured by a French privateer 30 leagues west of the Naze of Norway, on 15 July 1798. [AJ.2637]

STIRLING, GEORGE, husband of Mary Logan, in King's Crown, Old Deer, a member of the Aberdeenshire Militia in 1807. [ACA.AS.AMI.6.1.1]

STIRLING, GILBERT, schoolmaster at Cruden, testament, 3 July 1745, Comm. Aberdeen. [NRS]

STONE, JOHN, a shipmaster in Fraserburgh, testament, 28 February 1732, Comm. Aberdeen. [NRS]

STRACHAN, JAMES, master of the Prince Charles of Peterhead trading between Aberdeen, Newcastle, and Veere, in 1750- 1751. [AJ.149/161/162]; master of the Mayflower of Peterhead trading between Aberdeen, Kirkcaldy, Prestonpans and Newcastle, in 1750-1752. [NRS.E504.13/.4]

STUART, JOSEPH, a line manager aboard the whaling ship Robert of Peterhead off Greenland and the Davis Straits in 1794. [NRS.E508.94.8.10]

SUTOR, ANDREW, a seaman in Peterhead in 1696. [PPA.1]

SUTOR, EDWARD, a seaman in Peterhead in 1696. [PPA.1]

SUTOR, ..., master of the Ann of Peterhead at Aberdeen in 1750. [AJ.156]

SUTTER, JAMES, a whitefisher in Longhaven, Cruden, in 1696. [PPA.2]

SUTTER, JAMES, the younger, a whitefisher in Longhaven, Cruden, in 1696. [PPA.2]

THE PEOPLE OF BUCHAN, 1600-1799

SUTTER, JOHN, a whitefisher in Longhaven, Cruden, in 1696. [PPA.2]

SUTTER, J., master of the Active of Peterhead a whaler, in 1801. [HP.232]

SWAN, WILLIAM, born 1658, son of Reverend Alexander Swan and his wife Lean Leslie, was educated at King's College, Aberdeen, minister at Pitsligo from 1689 to 1716 when deposed as a Jacobite, Episcopalian priest of Fraserburgh from 1721 to 17--. died 1742, husband of Grizel Robertson, parents of Alexander and William. [SEC.527][F.6.234][NRS.GD124.6.188][JNES.38]

SYME, JOHN, minister at Lonmay, testament, 28 December 1752, Comm. Aberdeen. [NRS]

SYMON, WILLIAM, in Barhill, Rathven, testament, 10 May 1805, Comm. Aberdeen. [NRS]

TAES, WALTER, a shipmaster in Peterhead, testament, 20 June 1783, Comm. Aberdeen. [NRS]

TAIT, ALEXANDER, a whitefisher in Rathen, in 1696. [PPA.2]

TAIT, Robert, a whitefisher in Cairnbulg, Rathen, in 1696. [PPA.2]

TARRAS, DAVID, born 1691, son of William Tarras in Rattray, died in Peterhead on 18 February 1765, testament, 27 December 1765, Comm. Aberdeen. [NRS][Crimond gravestone]

TARVAS, ALEXANDER, a merchant in Fraserburgh, a Jacobite in 1745. [JNES.53]

TAYLOR, ALEXANDER, a sailor of the Robert of Peterhead whaling off Greenland or the Davis Straits in 1791. [NRS.E508.91.8]

TAYLOR, ANDREW, master of the William of Peterhead, a bark, in Aberdeen in 1610. [ASW.61]

TAYLOR, CHRISTIAN, died 6 October 1746. [Crimond gravestone]

THE PEOPLE OF BUCHAN, 1600-1799

TAYLOR, GEORGE, in Southgate, Peterhead, in 1741, reference in deed. [NRS.GD67.173]

TAYLOR, HUGH, born 8 May 1747, graduated MA from Marischal College, Aberdeen, in 1766, minister at New Deer from 1773 until 1830. [F.6.219]

TAYLOR, JAMES, born 1704, a sailor in Fraserburgh, died 28 May 1739, husband of Isobel Anderson born 1708, died 7 March 1764, parents of Christian, Elizabeth, and Isobel. [Fraserburgh Kirkton gravestone]

TAYLOR, JAMES, born 1797, a surgeon in Strichen, died in 1824. [AJ.28.5.1824]

TAYLOR, JOHN, a Jacobite in Fraserburgh in 1715. [JAB]

TAYLOR, JOHN, a ship-builder in Peterhead, testament, 27 January 1757, Comm. Aberdeen. [NRS]

TAYLOR, JOHN, a fresh or green man on the Robert of Peterhead whaling off Greenland or the Davis Straits in 1791. [NRS.E508.91.8]

TAYLOR, ROBERT, a seaman in Fraserburgh in 1696. [PA.2]

TAYLOR, WILLIAM, a seaman in Rosehearty, Pitsligo, in 1696. [PPA.2]

TAYLOR, WILLIAM, born ca1687, died August 1757, husband of Anne Lumsden, born 1684, died 13 June 1754, parents of William, John, and Margaret Taylor. [Aberdour gravestone]

TAYLOR, WILLIAM, an apprentice aboard the whaling ship Robert of Peterhead off Greenland and the Davis Straits in 1794. [NRS.E508.94.8.10]

TAYLOR, WILLIAM, a merchant in Peterhead, testament, 20 August 1795, Comm. Aberdeen. [NRS]

THE PEOPLE OF BUCHAN, 1600-1799

TAYLOR, WILLIAM, born 1708, graduated MA from King's College, Aberdeen, 1728, minister at New Deer from 1737, married Christian Gordon in 1737, parents of Mary, George, Alexander, John and Hugh his successor, died 29 April 1797, testament, 19 February 1800, Comm. Aberdeen. [NRS][F.6.219]

TAYLOR, WILLIAM, husband of Elizabeth Cowie, in Crimond, a sergeant of the Aberdeenshire Militia in 1804. [ACA.AS.AMI.6.1.1]

TAYLOR, ..., master of the Jean of Fraserburgh in Aberdeen in 1751. [AJ.192]

THOMSON, ALEXANDER, of Faichfield, Longside, son of Thomas Thomson of Faichfield and his wife Ann Gordon, a Jacobite in 1745. [JNES.53]

THOMSON, JAMES, in Peterhead, was served heir to his father William Thomson a shipmaster there, on 9 May 1764. [NRS.S/H]

THOMSON, JAMES, born 1732, died in March 1807, husband of Agnes Gordon, parents of Robert, James, George, Agnes, Ann and Mary. [Aberdour gravestone]

THOMSON, JAMES, in Stewartfield, Old Deer, testament, 17 August 1819, Comm. Aberdeen. [NRS]

THOMSON, JOHN, a Jacobite in Fraserburgh in 1715. [JNES.38]

THOMSON, PETER, in Strichen, letters, 1766-1768. [NRS.RH15.27.106]

THOMSON, THOMAS, of Cocklaw, died 25 October 1704, minister of Old Aberdeen, husband of Isobel Mercer, born 1634, died 3 March 1704. [VRA.206]

THOMSON, WILLIAM, master of the Anna of Peterhead trading with Norway in 1691, [NRS.E504.1.18]; a skipper in Peterhead, deeds, 1688, 1694, [NRS.RD2.69.178; RD4.75.413]; in Peterhead, 1696. [PPA.1]

THE PEOPLE OF BUCHAN, 1600-1799

THOMSON, WILLIAM, of Faichfield, parish of Longside, husband of Janet Gregory in 1696. [VRA.210]

THOMSON, WILLIAM, Cess Collector in Cullen, a Jacobite in 1715. [JNES.38]

THOMSON, WILLIAM, born 1746, died in New Aberdour on 19 October 1819, husband of Margaret Cowie, born 1755, died 28 July 1831, parents of Bettrich Thomson, born 1786, died 8 November 1856. [Aberdour gravestone]

TOD, WILLIAM, a merchant in Rouen, France, by 1652 in Fraserburgh. [RGS.X.46]

TORRY, PATRICK, Episcopalian priest of Peterhead from 1789 to 1837. [SEC]

TOUGH, ALEXANDER, master of the Anne of Peterhead was stranded near Banff when bound from Gothenburg to Veere in 1767. [AJ.992]

TRAIL, JAMES, born 1795, a surgeon, died in Peterhead in 1823. [AJ.2.6.1823]

TROUP, Captain WILLIAM, and ANN LESLIE, were married in Fraserburgh on 5 March 1791. [NRS.CH12.32.2]

TULLOCH, ALEXANDER, of Clerkhills in the parish of Peterhead in 1696. [VRA.207]

TURING, JAMES, born 1709, son of Sir John Turing, educated at King's College, Aberdeen, minister at Aberdour from September 1733 until his death on 19 October 1733. [F.6.210]

TYLER, JAMES, the elder, a whitefisher in Cairnbulg, Rathen, in 1696. [PPA.1]

TYLER, JAMES, the younger, a whitefisher in Cairnbulg, Rathen, in 1696. [PPA.1]

100

THE PEOPLE OF BUCHAN, 1600-1799

TYTLER, WILLIAM, jr., in Peterhead, was served heir to his mother Jean Stephen, wife of William Tytler sr. a wright in Peterhead, in August 1808. [NRS.S/H]

UDNY, THOMAS, minister at Strichen, testament, 12 November 1782, Comm. Aberdeen. [NRS]

URQUHART, GEORGE, a skipper in Fraserburgh, trading in conjunction with his brother Patrick Urquhart a merchant in Fraserburgh, with the Carolinas, master of the Hope in 1744, George died on the return voyage. [NRS.AC9.1605]

URQUHART, JAMES, born 1667, a skipper in Fraserburgh, died 27 December 1741. [Fraserburgh gravestone]

URQUHART, JAMES, a merchant and bailie of Fraserburgh, testament, 7 December 1730, Comm. Aberdeen. [NRS]

URQUHART, PATRICK, a merchant in Fraserburgh, who traded with the Carolinas in 1744, testament, 20 June 1783, Comm. Aberdeen. [NRS][NRS.AC9.1605]

URQUHART, WILLIAM, a merchant in Fraserburgh, a Jacobite in 1715. [JNES.39]

URQUHART, WILLIAM, a merchant and bailie of Fraserburgh, testament, 19 March 1776, Comm. Aberdeen. [NRS]

URQUHART, WILLIAM, farm servant at Banks in the parish of Strichen, testament, 6 August 1823, Comm. Aberdeen. [NRS]

VARE, ALEXANDER, a barber in Rosehearty, and Sophia Hepburn from near the Kirk of Pitsligo, were married in Fraserburgh on 11 July 1793. [NRS.CH12.32.2]

VOLUM, ANN, widow of Andrew Dargue a sailor in Peterhead, was served heir to her father Thomas Vollum a shipmaster there, on 21 November 1760. [NRS.S/H]

THE PEOPLE OF BUCHAN, 1600-1799

VOLUM, JAMES, a surgeon, son of William Volum, a sailor in Harbour Street, Peterhead, and his wife Ann Strachan, a Jacobite in 1745, fled abroad in 1746, returned, was served heir to his father William Volum a sailor there, on 25 March 1768, [NRS.S/H]; married Mary Hay, died in Peterhead in 1786. [JNES.55]

VOLUM, JANET, wife of William Brodie a sailor at Bullersbuchan, was served heir to her father Thomas Volum a shipmaster in Peterhead, on 21 December 1760. [NRS.S/H]

VOLUM, JEAN, in Peterhead, wife of James Hector a mason in Aberdeen, was served heir to her father Thomas Volum a shipmaster in Peterhead, on 21 November 1760, [NRS.S/H]; a testament, 28 October 1799. [NRS]

VOLUM, THOMAS, a skipper in Peterhead, dead by 1760. [NRS.S/H]

VOLUM, WILLIAM, master of the Mayflower of Peterhead trading between Grangepans and Aberdeen in 1742; trading with Bergen, Sinfjord, and Newcastle in 1749-1750. [NRS.E504.1.1/3]

VOLUM, WILLIAM, a skipper in Peterhead, son of James Volum a surgeon in Peterhead, a sasine, 1798, master of the Greenland whaler Enterprise of Peterhead in 1804. [NRS.RS.Aberdeen.1822][TWY2][HP.232]

WALKER, ANDREW, a skipper in Colliston, Slains, in 1696. [PPA.1]

WALKER, ISOBEL, in Strichen, testament, 28 March 1811, Comm. Aberdeen. [NRS]

WALKER, JAMES, a whitefisher in Bullarsbuchan, Cruden, in 1696. [PPA.2]

WALKER, JAMES, a seaman in Fraserburgh, a deed, 1696. [NRS.RD4.79.1035]

THE PEOPLE OF BUCHAN, 1600-1799

WALKER, JAMES, son of James Walker a merchant in Peterhead, graduated MA from Marischal College, Aberdeen, in 1723, minister at Peterhead from 1739 until his death on 1 January 1763, husband of [1] Janet Gordon, [2] Elizabeth Innes. [F.6.232]; testament, 15 June 1763, Comm. Aberdeen. [NRS]

WALKER, JAMES, son of Alexander Walker in Fraserburgh, was educated at Marischal College, Aberdeen, from 1785 to 1789, graduated MA, later became Bishop of Edinburgh. [MCA]

WALKER, JOHN, a seaman in Fraserburgh in 1696. [PPA.2]

WALKER, JOHN, in Peterhead, a bond, 1698. [NRS.GD244.1.269]

WALKER, JOHN, and Jane Duncan, both in Fraserburgh, were married there on 6 October 1799. [Fraserburgh Episcopal records]

WALKER, JOHN, a feuar in Fraserburgh, testament, 11 March 1808, Comm. Aberdeen. [NRS]

WALKER, MARGARET, in Peterhead, testament, 15 November 1764, Comm. Aberdeen. [NRS]

WALKER, ROBERT, a fresh or green man on the Robert of Peterhead whaling off Greenland or the Davis Straits in 1791. [NRS.E508.91.8]

WALKER, ROBERT, born 1774 in Colliston, a crewman of the herring buss Polly of Peterhead in 1792. [NRS.E508.94.9.56]

WALKER, WILLIAM, Episcopalian priest of Fraserburgh from 1734 to 1766. [SEC.527]

WALKER, WILLIAM, a skipper in Fraserburgh, a sasine, 1783. [NRS.RS.Aberdeen.226]

WALLACE, JOHN, in Southgate, Peterhead, in 1741, reference in deed. [NRS.GD67.173]

THE PEOPLE OF BUCHAN, 1600-1799

WALLACE, JOHN, in Cothill, Slains, testament, 17 June 1791, Comm. Aberdeen. [NRS]

WALLACE, JOHN, a watchmaker, and Mary Hay, were married in Fraserburgh on 31 August 1800. [NRS.CH12.32.2]

WATERSTON, JAMES, a skipper in Fraserburgh, a deed, 1675. [NRS.RD4.38.68]; a deed, 1714. [NRS.RD4.114.44]

WATERSTON, JOHN, master of the Swan of Fraserburgh, trading between Norway and Aberdeen in 1683. [NRS.E72.1.9/11]; a skipper in Fraserburgh in 1696. [PPA.2]

WATSON, ANDREW, a bailie of Peterhead in 1680. [NRS.GD70.242]

WATSON, JAMES, of Strichen, a letter, 1767. [NRS.RH15.27.118]

WATSON, JANET, in Longside, testament, 24 July 1750, Comm. Aberdeen. [NRS]

WATSON, JOHN, in Strichen House, letters, 1767-1768. [NRS.RH15.27.118]

WATSON, JOSEPH, son of William Watson tacksman of Caweyford, parish of Old Deer, was apprenticed to Alexander Mitchell a merchant in Aberdeen, for 4 years, 22 June 1785. Cautioner was John Todd a weaver in Pitmark House, Old Deer. [ACA]

WATT, ALEXANDER, from New Deer, settled in Canada, heir to his mother Isabella Norrie or Watt in Auchreddie, Aberdeenshire, [NRS.S/H.1836]

WATT, ANDREW, the elder, a seaman in Aberdour in 1696. [PPA.2]

WATT, ANDREW, the younger, a seaman in Aberdour in 1696. [PPA.2ew Deer gravestone]

THE PEOPLE OF BUCHAN, 1600-1799

WATT, GEORGE, in the Mains of Cairnbulg, testament, 28 December 1791, Comm. Aberdeen. [NRS]

WATT, JAMES, in Rathen, testament, 4 July 1752, Comm. Aberdeen. [NRS]

WATT, JOHN, the elder, a seaman in Aberdour in 1696. [PPA.2]

WATT, JOHN, the younger, a seaman in Aberdour in 1696. [PPA.2]

WATT, JOHN, born 1707, late in Bridgefoot, died 12 January 1776, husband of Elspet Gray, born 1703, died 4 June 1792. [New Deer gravestone]

WATT, ROBERT, master of the sloop Experiment of Peterhead in 1766. [AJ.943]

WATT, WILLIAM, a seaman in Aberdour in 1696. [PPA.2]

WATT, WILLIAM, son of William Watt at the Waulkmilne of Strichen, testament, 29 April 1794, Comm. Aberdeen. [NRS]

WATT, WILLIAM, a merchant in New Pitsligo, testament, 22 August 1815, Comm. Aberdeen. [NRS]

WEBSTER, ALEXANDER, born 1719, died 13 January 1799, husband of Jean Chalmers, born 1718, died 28 December 1775, in Cairns of Auchmingzel, parents of Isabel born 1763 died 12 May 1776, M argaret born 1754, died 29 November 1776, Charles, born 1761 or 1767, died 12 January 1787, John born 1756, died 28 December 1818. [New Deer gravestone]

WEBSTER, GEORGE, a merchant in Strichen, testament, 5 June 1819, Comm. Aberdeen. [NRS]

WEBSTER, JAMES, in Elles Hill, husband of Janet Trail, born 1740, died 27 October 1789. [New Deer gravestone]

WEBSTER, JOHN, MA, minister at New Deer from 1707 until 1720, later at Cruden, testaments, 29 March 1743 and 23 July 1752, Comm. Aberdeen. [NRS][F.6.219]

THE PEOPLE OF BUCHAN, 1600-1799

WEBSTER, JOHN, born 27 August 1740, died in June 1788, husband of Jean Ironside. [New Deer gravestone]

WEBSTER, JOHN, late in the Mills of Fraserburgh, in Crossburntland, testament, 1 February 1772, Comm. Aberdeen. [NRS]

WEBSTER, ROBERT, born 1705, farmer in Wittenshill, died 29 September 1767, husband of Janet Henderson, born 1691, died 10 May 1780. [New Deer gravestone]

WELLS, GEORGE, born 1715, died at sea on 15 May 1790, husband of Elisabeth Watson, born 1729, died in Crossgates of Coburty in August 1776, parents of Isobel Wells, born 1751, died 15 May 1776. [Aberdour gravestone]

WELLS, JAMES, in Milne of Fishrie, husband of Anna White, born 1702, died 17 January 1745, parents of Mary, born 1740, died 20 August 1741, and John, born 1733, died 28 April 1753. [Aberdour gravestone]

WEMYSS, JANET, relict of Thomas Ogilvie a litster in Fraserburgh, testament, 7 February 1737, Comm. Aberdeen. [NRS]

WEMYSS, JOHN, late tacksman of the Mains of Aberdour, testament, 6 January 1749, Comm. Aberdeen. [NRS]

WEST, JAMES, born 1699, died on the Shore of Auchmeddan on 4 January 1759, a church Elder, husband of Mary Wat, born 1698, died 6 August 1763. [Aberdour gravestone]

WEST, JOHN, the elder, a seaman in Aberdour in 1696. [PPA.2]

WEST, JOHN, the younger, a seaman in Aberdour in 1696. [PPA.2]

WEST, JOHN, the youngest, a seaman in Aberdour in 1696. [PPA.2]

WEST, JOHN, born 1690s, died 11 March 1767, husband of Margaret Wilson, died 17 May 174-, parents of Lieutenant John West. [Aberdour gravestone]

THE PEOPLE OF BUCHAN, 1600-1799

WEST, WILLIAM, the elder, a seaman in Aberdour in 1696. [PPA.2]

WEST, WILLIAM, born 1680, died 2 December 1756, father of John West. [Aberdour gravestone]

WHYTE, ALEXANDER, a whitefisher in Rathen in 1696. [PPA.1]

WHITE, ALEXANDER, born 1691, died 11 November 1741, husband of Janet Gall, born 1694, died 9 January 1745, in Dubfoord, parents of William [1730-1801], Margery, and Margaret. [Aberdour gravestone]

WHYTE, ANDREW, master of the Christian of Cairnbulg trading between Kirkcaldy and Aberdeen in 1751. [NRS.E504.1.4]; from Fraserburgh to Aberdeen in 1758. [AJ.542]

WHYTE, JAMES, Episcopalian priest of Strichen, 1669-1689, and 1694-1699. [SEC.534]

WHYTE, GEORGE, born 1745, a weaver in Auchmeddan, died 19 February 1797, his sister Isabella Whyte, born 1770, died in Auchmeddan on 21 October 1855. [Aberdour gravestone]

WHYTE, JAMES, senior, a Jacobite in Fraserburgh in 1715. [JNES.39]

WHITE, JOHN, minister of Aberdour from 1691 until 1694. [F.B.210]

WHITE, PATRICK, a tidesman in Peterhead, testament, 2 May 1777, Comm. Aberdeen. [NRS]

WHYTE, Captain WILLIAM, a skipper in Fraserburgh, husband of Christian Livingston, a sasine, 1790, [NRS.RS.Aberdeen.858]; testament, 14 June 1792, Comm. Aberdeen. [NRS]

WHITE, WILLIAM, from Fraserburgh, a shopkeeper in Charleston, South Carolina, probate 19 July 1793, Charleston.

THE PEOPLE OF BUCHAN, 1600-1799

WILDGOOSE, JAMES, son of John Wildgoose in Old Deer, was apprenticed to Colin Allan a goldsmith in Aberdeen for 7 years, 1749. [ACA]

WILDGOOSE, JAMES, in Meikletoun of Slains, son of Alexander Wildgose in Ward of Slains, testament, 29 February 1776, Comm. Aberdeen. [NRS]

WILDGOOSE, THOMAS, a weaver in Peterhead, testament, 26 May 1801, Comm. Aberdeen. [NRS]

WILL, MATTHEW, master of the Grace of God of Peterhead trading between Leith and Aberdeen in 1613. [ASW.75]

WILLIAMSON, JAMES, in St Fergus, dead by 1838, grand-father of James Williamson a mason in Canada. [NRS.S/H]

WILSON, ALEXANDER, a merchant in Fraserburgh, a sasine, 1676. [NRS.GD1.38.62]

WILSON, ALEXANDER, [1], a seaman in Rosehearty, Pitsligo, in 1696. [PPA.2]

WILSON, ALEXANDER, [2], a seaman in Rosehearty, Pitsligo, in 1696. [PPA.2]

WILSON, ALEXANDER, in Fraserburgh, a letter, 1768. [NRS.CH12.23.1337]

WILSON, ALEXANDER, and Ann Pirie, both in Fraserburgh, were married there on 31 December 1796. [NRS.CH12.32.2]

WILSON, ANDREW, [1], a seaman in Rosehearty, Pitsligo, in 1696. [PPA.2]

WILSON, ANDREW, [2], a seaman in Rosehearty, Pitsligo, in 1696. [PPA.2]

WILSON, ANNIE, born 1755, widow of William Fraser minister of Tyrie, died in Aberdeen in 1835. [AJ.13.3.1835]

THE PEOPLE OF BUCHAN, 1600-1799

WILSON, CECILIA, in Strichen, letters, 1766-1768. [NRS.RH15.27.117]

WILSON, Dr DAVID, a physician in Peterhead, son of James Wilson of Finzeach, a disposition, 1771. [NRS.GD52.761]; testament, 15 November 1791, Comm. Aberdeen. [NRS]

WILSON, GEORGE, master of the Diligence of Peterhead trading between Danzig and Aberdeen in 1742; trading between Bumblefiord and Aberdeen in 1743; from Rotterdam to Aberdeen in 1743. [NRS.E504.1.1]

WILSON, JAMES, a merchant in Fraserburgh, a memorial, 1715. [NRS.GD220.6.1752.11]

WILSON, JAMES, a sailor in Peterhead, was jailed for perjury in 1768. [AJ.1046]

WILSON, JOHN, a seaman in Rosehearty, Pitsligo, in 1696. [PPA.2]

WILSON, J., a farm servant in Buchan, dead by 1834, father of John Wilson a millwright in New York. [NRS.S/H]

WILSON, MARGARET, daughter of Alexander Wilson of Fornest, a merchant in Fraserburgh, testament, 29 June 1769, Comm. Aberdeen. [NRS]

WILSON, ROBERT, owner of the Mill of Adziel, parish of Strichen, 1770. [NRS.E106.36.5]

WOOD, GEORGE, a skipper in Peterhead, a deed, 1682. [NRS.RD4.50.749]

WOOD, JAMES, master of the Thomas and Mary of Peterhead trading between Aberdeen and Trontheim in 1743; trading between Nessham and Aberdeen in 1743; from Newcastle to Aberdeen in 1743. [NRS.E504.1.1]; trading between trading between Aberdeen and Rotterdam in 1749, [NRS.E504.1.3]; trading between Aberdeen, Peterhead, and Norway in 1751. [AJ.172/192]; trading with Lisbon, Oporto, Christiansands,

Aberdeen and Bumblefjord, and Flekkefjord in 1751.
[NRS.E504.1.4]; in Lisbon in 1754, [AJ.354]; trading between
Veere and Aberdeen in 1755. [AJ.386]

WOOD, JOHN, master of the Thomas and Mary of Peterhead
trading with Newcastle in 1751. [NRS.E504.1.4]

WOOD, WILLIAM, a shoemaker in Rosehearty, testaments, 11
November 1742, and 17 January 1745, Comm. Aberdeen. [NRS]

YOOL, ALEXANDER, a shipmaster in Fraserburgh, later mariner on
the Lord Saltoun of Fraserburgh, testament, 1 November 1822,
Comm. Aberdeen. [NRS]

YOUNG, ALEXANDER, husband of Ann Henderson, in Old Deer, a
member of the Aberdeenshire Militia in 1807. [ACA.AS.AMI.6.1.1]

YOUNG, JAMES, son of James Young in New Mill of Crimond, was
apprenticed to William Law a baker in Aberdeen, for 5 years, 4
November 1785. [ACA]

YOUNG, JOHN, master of the Fortune of Peterhead in Aberdeen
in 1661, [ASW.461]; master of the Charles of Peterhead, deeds,
1684, 1688. [NRS.RD4.64.417; RD2.69.178]

YOUNGSON, ANDREW, born 1727 in New Deer, graduated MA
from King's College, Aberdeen, in 1747, minister at Aberdour
from {1766 until his death in 1801. Husband of {1} Mary Taylor, {2}
Agnes Anderson, father of Christian, Alexander, William, James,
Agnes Margaret, Thomas, and Andrew. [F.6.210]

Printed in the USA
CPSIA information can be obtained
at www.ICGtesting.com
JSHW050516181123
52125JS00016B/167